Asian Costumes and Textiles

To my wife Biki, who like Ulysses
loves travelling.

Hecuba returned to the palace, dispatching her servants
To call the noblewomen of the city,
Then went alone to the geranium-fragrant room
Where the covering cloths were kept, all embroidered.
Here were a thousand motifs, the handiwork of Sidonese women,
Cloths brought from Sidon by god-like Alexandros
When he abducted Helen to carry her
Over the wide sea, and then be home.
Hecuba chose the biggest, most beautiful cloth
To offer Athena; it shone like a star
At the bottom of the chest.

Homer (*The Iliad, VI*)

Asian Costumes and Textiles

from the Bosphorus to Fujiyama

The Zaira and Marcel Mis Collection

Introduction by
Mary Hunt Kahlenberg

Contributions by
Valérie Berinstain, Claudine Delecourt,
Mary Hunt Kahlenberg and Frieda Sorber

Photos by
Mauro Magliani

Stylist
Sandrard

SKIRA

Front Cover
Uzbekistan
Men's coat
Silk and cotton, 144 × 76 cm

Back Cover
Japan
*Woollen fire coat (*kajibaori*)*
Silk and metal thread, 97 × 125 cm

Flyleaves
Sultan's view of the Bosphorus from the Palace
of Topkapi (photo by Izzet Keribar)

View of Mount Fuji

Scientific Editor
Eric Ghysels

Art Director
Marcello Francone

Editorial Coordination
Marzia Branca

Editing and Layout
Claudio Nasso
Serena Parini
Antonio Carminati

First published in Italy in 2001 by
Skira Editore S.p.A.
Palazzo Casati Stampa
via Torino 61
20123 Milano
Italy

Printed and bound in Italy. First edition

ISBN 88-8118-971-2

Distributed in North America and Latin America
by Rizzoli International Publications, Inc.
through St. Martin's Press,
175 Fifth Avenue, New York, NY 10010.
Distributed elsewhere in the world
by Thames and Hudson Ltd.,
181a High Holborn, London WC1V 7QX,
United Kingdom

Acknowledgments

We are profoundly grateful to the many people who often went far out of their way in order to help us to produce this book. The search for the best costumes and their final selection necessitated a great deal of time-consuming discussions and involved the aid and co-operation of a large number of persons. We would like to acknowledge the assistance of the following in particular, Mary Hunt Kahlenberg author, consultant and adviser in antique and ethnographic textiles, helped us extensively with her knowledge and expertise. She graciously gave up two days of a holiday trip to Paris with her husband Robert to finalize the Introduction and the chapter on South-East Asia. Colette Ghysels, who with her eagle eye helped us to start our collection and with her advice taught us how to pick out the better pieces. Very often Colette gave us the opportunity to be the first to view her discoveries, which made a major contribution towards enriching our collection with some high-quality and rare pieces. We recall with gratitude the long late evenings she spent with her husband Jean-Pierre helping us to make the improvements they found necessary to the book. The cheerful team made up of Jacqueline De Bolle, Frieda Sorber and Agnès Asbil, who took six hundred amateur photos and selected, prepared and annotated the costumes for the book, and in particular Frieda Sorber, curator of the Antwerp Costume and Textile Museum, for her introduction to the chapter on the Middle East. Valérie Berinstain, ex-curator of the AEDTA Asiatic Textile Collection, whose valuable knowledge was indispensable in the drafting of the chapters on Central Asia and India. Claudine Delecourt, instructor and lecturer at the Royal Art and History Museum of Brussels, who provided very useful and expert information for the chapter devoted to the Far East. Mauro Magliani, our photographer, for his good-humoured patience and his constant endeavours to produce quality results. Our long-standing friend Sandrard, whose skill helped to enhance the originality of the photographs. Éric Ghysels, from Skira, who convinced us of the importance of publishing a book of our collection and who duly honoured his commitment to ensure that the book would be published in the best possible conditions. Anne van Cutsem, who for many years has helped us to organize our collection. Leslie Grace, who provided useful information on Burmese garments. Jean Rividi, who devoted his valuable time to translating many of the texts into English. Florence De Brier, our faithful assistant, who spent countless hours typing and retyping the translations and captions we were constantly trying to improve. Marc Ghysels, who made everyone's life so much easier by organizing the computer side of the project for us. Izzet Keribar, from Istanbul, who provided the superb shot of the Bosphorus seen from the Palace of Topkapi. Our cousin Mati Rodrik, from Istanbul, whose generous hospitality and assistance enabled us to find some of the best pieces in our Ottoman collection. The Hutheesing family from Ahmedabad, for their hospitality and assistance in enabling us to meet important collectors of their acquaintance. Numerous leading dealers from all over the world and in particular Maharukh Desai, the late Manubai from Ahmedabad, J. Holmgren, A. Spertus, Sarajo, Junnaa Wroblewski, Ziya Aykaç Muhlis Günbatti together with many others who remain anonymous but will recognize themselves. A.R. Clarke, who conscientiously revised the final English text. Last, but no means least, the members of our more immediate family, in particular our son Alain and our daughter Natasha, who were always available to stand in for us when necessary.

Marcel and Zaira Mis

Most of the costumes and textiles in this book date from the second half of the nineteenth century, but a few of them are from the eighteenth century or from the beginning of the twentieth. Since precise dates are not available for many of the traditional costumes, we preferred to leave them out completely. The names and frontiers of many countries were changed during the twentieth century, and we felt it would be historically more correct to retain the original attribution of some items.
In the section Near East, for Turkey, the pieces illustrated are regarded as examples of Ottoman handicrafts as they date from before 1923.
Pakistan and Bangladesh have not been indicated as such, since the illustrated pieces date from well before 1947, when these territories were part of India.

Contents

Zaira Mis

How a Collection Became a Passion

Everything began with a love story: first our own, which was born in the shadow of the Brussels Atomium in 1958, when we were barely twenty years old. This was to be followed by a shared love of exotic trips, colourful markets, sumptuous materials and unfamiliar weaving techniques, a love for which I have to thank my husband Marcel, a textile engineer. In the course of all our trips this love developed into a veritable passion, which led to the creation of our collection.

Originally, it was not our intention to start a collection. We merely derived enormous pleasure from buying exotic souvenirs, giving unusual gifts, having a beautiful scarf to drape round one's shoulder, replacing a very ordinary cloth bag by a delightful embroidered pouch or bringing our children those amusing Peruvian hats to protect the ears. The striped poncho I found in Chichicastegnango market in Guatemala came in very useful in Ladakh and Tibet, where it afforded protection against the icy cold of the evenings in Leh and Hemis. Thanks to the creative imagination of Sandrard and his skill in concealing holes and signs of wear, the green and gold sarong bought from a young woman on the sun-soaked beach of Trincomalee in Sri Lanka turned into a charming dress which, when decorated with a red pompom from a piece of Meo headgear, prompted general admiration in all who saw it.

However, we were soon bitten by the bug… . We started by falling for a ceremonial costume, a Japanese fireman's jacket, a Cameroun huntsman's tunic covered with gri-gri amulets. Then we learnt to be more choosy, looking for pieces that were old but in good condition, garments that were traditional but out of the ordinaly. Trying to find rare, even unique items, things that were not yet in our collection became a need, an obsession, but also a truly exciting hobby.

We had incredible adventures and, occasionally, found ourselves in uncomfortable situations in our attempts to get close to the inhabitants of remote villages in their traditional garments. In northern Thailand, we covered many miles on foot through fields, watercourses and paths under a relentless sun, sipping Coca-Cola through a straw to avoid dehydration. In Bolivia we found ourselves speeding across Lake Titicaca in an unlit outboard motorboat, in the middle of a starless night, in order to be in a fishing village at daybreak. One had to be young and a little reckless to venture through an Indonesian forest by bemo, a kind of simple motorcycle-cum-taxi, in order to visit the home of a stranger who wanted to show us some unusual costumes.

Our collection is also due to the magnificent selections made by antique dealers in the countries we have visited. We are familiar figures in the bazaar of Istanbul. At Ahmadabad in Gujarat, our friends the Hutheesings took us to the shop of the late Manubai, who helped to enrich the two largest collections of Indian textiles in the world: that of the local textile museum and that of Krishna Riboud, who died recently. There we chose magnificent kanthas and charming folk costumes covered in bright-coloured embroidery, with micas and mirrors reflecting the light. Then there are the travelling dealers who regularly go to these distant regions and know of our passionate interest in what they find there.

Fully taken up with our other activities, we have devoted our evenings and even nights to welcoming these travellers in order to view and purchase

Ottoman Empire (Turkey)

From left to right:
Cotton muslin scarf embroidered with silver strips and threads in floral motifs.
150 × 135 cm

Linen bath towel (havlu) *embroidered at both ends with floral and geometric motifs in coloured silk and silver threads.*
270 × 300 cm

their offerings. Holidays have been sacrificed to index and catalogue our textiles. Exhibitions and ethnographic museums hold no more mysteries for us and are our preferred destinations during our travels. It is in this way that we have developed an appreciation of the finest qualities of the objects we discover.

We can now distinguish between the genuine and the bogus and are able to gauge the special characteristics of certain fibres and materials, the delicacy of an embroidery, the complexity of certain weaves, the incredible dyeing techniques employed, the wide range of designs, the time and love – again and again – that these anonymous craftsmen have invested in their creations.

All of the items in our possession can tell a story – that of the traditions, culture, community or caste of their owners, and sometimes that of their trade or status in life. They have been worn and admired at festivities or colourful ceremonies and frequently they have been handed down from generation to generation. It is difficult to suppress a feeling of considerable emotion when looking at a small Kutch child's robe or a resplendent royal garment.

This book, which is the fruit of much hard work but was created with a large measure of enthusiasm, aims to share the pleasure we experienced in discovering what we regard as our wonders. However, despite our greatest efforts, which meant that the text was read and re-read countless times, it will doubtless still contain flaws, omissions or inaccuracies, for which we beg the reader's indulgence.

Far from being restricted to certain countries, regions or techniques, our collection, which is the result of a labour of love and has been built up empirically in the course of our travels, contains examples from all over the world and includes textile objects other than clothes such as headgear, shoes, belts and jewellery. We have been inspired by our feelings and by an instinctive desire to preserve for posterity these extraordinary witnesses to the past, especially since they are among those that are sought after by most lovers of antiques.

Clothes, and textiles in general, are fragile; very few survive for centuries and even fewer survive in good condition. There are several reasons for this: the way of life of the societies in which they were created and the changes, migrations and even disappearance of the peoples who wore them, but also natural phenomena, political events and, more importantly, economic factors, which leave little room for patient, manual work. Bearing this in mind, we shall continue to enrich our collection with the same curiosity, the same element of folly and the same passion which have been features of our activities since their inception.

Syria
*Four tulip-shaped silk and metal thread
purses woven in tapestry (kilim) weave
with floral motifs.*
16 × 11 cm

Marcel Mis

A Homage to the Skills of the Past

As a textile engineer and fashion designer, I knew very little about Asian clothes, and during my first trip to India, while visiting the Calico Museum of Ahmedabad, I was staggered by the profusion of varieties of textiles and the wide range of techniques used to manufacture items of clothing. They were largely new to me, and from that day on, my wife and I decided to search out, collect and preserve traditional costumes and textiles.

We found everything irresistible – the wall hangings, shawls, scarves, blouses, skirts, dresses and robes, brilliantly coloured and beautifully designed, superbly decorated with embroideries, applications, mirrors, shells and beads. These costumes and textiles enable us to wander through the history of the world, from the rise of civilizations to the fall of empires, through wars, conquests, migrations and commercial exchanges with a blend of diverse cultures, legends and religions. The fabrics, designs, motifs, weaves, embroideries and ornaments are part of the rich, mysterious heritage of these cultures. Each textile is an example of the cultural peculiarities of its region of origin. In Palestine, as in Turkistan, Burma, India, the Indonesian islands, China and Japan, we find communities and castes living side by side in peace or at war and expressing their differences through colour, costumes and jewellery.

Very often distant countries and cultures, knowing nothing of each other's existence, employed similar spinning, weaving, dyeing and embroidering techniques, even with similar costume designs.

It was the collector's good fortune to observe, examine and compare these techniques as applied to similar animal and vegetable raw materials, which belong to all cultures, including our own.

In a desire to share with others our delight in the broad variety of textiles and costumes in our collection, we decided to produce this book, which is intended as a tribute to all those – men, women, children and families – who worked hard to make all these beautiful objects, while remaining anonymous; a tribute to their patience and generosity in conveying their knowledge, methods and skills through the generations, with due acknowledgement of the technical processes used, frequently under difficult conditions, by the hand-loom weavers, block printers, *ikat* and resist dyers, painters and nimble-fingered embroiderers from the towns and villages of all these distant civilizations. We would like to help ensure that the crafts and skills of these weavers, dyers and embroiderers withstand the ever-present threat to their existence and will be kept alive for future generations.

Uzbek
Leather and silk velvet boots with applications of silver and silk ornaments; lining is in ikatted silk.
43 × 11 cm
Bukhara silk shawl with gold floral embroideries at each end.
232 × 27.5 cm

Mary Hunt Kahlenberg

Looking in and out

As those who know them personally will attest, when Zaira and Marcel Mis consider the acquisition of a costume for their outstanding collection, their discussions are intense but brief. So on a recent trip to visit them at their home, I was somewhat surprised to learn that what seems like an almost effortless meeting of minds is anything but a simple process. In fact, they reach agreement only after travelling surprisingly divergent roads. Marcel studies a textile at close range, judging its attention to detail, the intricacy of the techniques used and the quality of the craftsmanship. In contrast, Zaira approaches a potential acquisition by viewing it as a single image. She weighs its overall aesthetic, asking herself whether the article in question delivers a powerful and lasting impression. Quickly debating the merits of a textile from these very different points of view, Zaira and Marcel decide to acquire the piece only if and when it meets the exacting criteria set by each of them.

How and why collections that of the Mises are built is a complex matter. A collection is individualistic by nature, yet also very much the result of the collectors' time and place. The formation of the Mis costume collection provides an excellent example of how intellectual ideas, personal feelings and the tenor of the times meet at a single point.

Zaira and Marcel pursue two different but compatible careers. Originally from Turkey, Marcel heads a company that creates well-designed and finely made women's clothing. Zaira, who hails from Italy, owns and directs a contemporary art gallery. As a result of their different professions, each brings a definite perspective to collecting. Some decisions seem natural considering their education and backgrounds. Others are the result of their personal natures. But for every costume or textile that they add to their collection, both Zaira and Marcel insist that the item possess an innate quality, a core of visceral feeling. The Mises call this "human-ness."

Although "human-ness" does not appear in a dictionary, the meaning of the term is clear. By their very nature costumes – or in today's terminology, clothes – are an intimate expression of the wearer. Clothes hug, shield and advertise the body. Both a personal expression and a public display, clothes connect the wearer to his or her physical environment on a daily basis – think of a fireman's protective coat, a chief's symbolic hat or a dinner jacket. Especially for occasions of importance such as a wedding or funeral, clothes broadcast intention and frequently dictate behaviour. Even when we view these clothes several hundred years after they were made and worn, clothes – which now have become known as costumes in a collector's parlance – impart this sense of "human-ness" to a viewer. Our mind easily imagines the wearer at work in a rice paddy or bowing at a temple or swaying amid torchlight at a ceremonial dance.

"Human-ness": what exactly is this efficacious quality and how is it transmitted? The power of an object to affect us is accentuated by its physical qualities. If we can touch a textile, hold it in our hands, turn it inside out, become familiar with the subtleties of its texture, the manner of its workmanship and even the peculiarities of its assemblage, we begin to connect with its origins. Initially this is a mental exercise. We are looking for information. Next we move beyond the physical qualities of the textile to its contextual aspects. We measure our knowledge of its history

India, Bengal
Kantha, *cotton coverlet from Faridpur (Sujni). Quilted embroidery shows popular scenes of daily life and familiar animals: cows, birds, peacocks, elephants, fish, horses, etc… and the five-lotus motif.*
230 × 118 cm

and the culture that produced it, and we look for information about the symbolism of its motifs or overall form.

Eventually this search brings us back to our physical contact with the textile, and we begin to feel an untenable link with the textile and its past. More strongly than before, we understand that a costume is not born into the world as an orphan. The garment was a product of its maker and the expression of its wearer. We may never know exactly how these garments played themselves out in the life of their original owners. But the "humanness" of the textile continues to resonate, asking us many questions and tantalizing us with possible answers. Was the bride happy on the day she wore her wedding dress? Did the fireman rescue a child from the blazing home? We receive no definite answers, of course, but we have definitely communicated with the past.

Caring for a collection of costumes is rich with emotion, physical and intellectual pleasures. The Mises, both late-night people, frequently head up to the beautiful gallery on the third floor of their home at 10 or 11 p.m. The two-room space is lined with diamond-shaped glass panels crafted by an Italian cabinet-maker. In the first room, costumes hang from rods or are folded carefully on shelves. The second room is more of a workroom, with costumes displayed on mannequins or lying on tables. Here the Mises and their many visitors relax and examine the textiles at close range, noting affinities like the ikat technique in its various forms from Afghanistan to the Philippines, or observing the continuity of the running diamond design from southern China to the island of Timor in the eastern Indonesian archipelago. No matter how casual this contact may be with the textiles, the Mises continue to acquire a growth of knowledge and intuitive understanding about their collection. The power of the textiles bypasses the literal constructions of language. Just touching the costumes is a profound experience for the Mises. They are changed without words.

In particular, Marcel Mis marvels at the workmanship of these garments. This is a totally different reality from the commercial world of fashion that is his daily life, reflecting a bygone world where time and costs are not linked. Instead, Marcel recognizes a connection between the level of skill required to fashion the textile and knowledge of traditional methods. Both must be there for the costume to meet a community standard. The skill may be passed from mother to daughter or father to son, usually by a non-verbal method relying on imitation by the child. The skill level

of many of these garments and their decorations is no longer attainable. This is not because the technology no longer exists. In many cases, the technology is extremely simple: embroidery requires only a needle and thread, and the most complex ikat pattern can be accomplished on a very basic loom. Everything could be easily reproduced if it was not for the one thing that is lacking in today's world: time; not just time to create the work, but the time involved in acquiring the skill to produce it.

This fact is not lost on a contemporary observer. An attraction to material of earlier times and different cultures is partially a result of the shift in our perception of time. Time is constant but *how* we view time changes our attitude towards it. When we look at a double *ikat geringsing* textile from Bali or a finely embroidered jacket from Sumatra, we tend to compare the time required to create the textile with a task we might accomplish within the same time. Perhaps it took three years to tie and dye the Balinese *geringsing*, the efforts of one woman working on and off as the demands of farming, family and the seasons permitted. What happened in her life during those years? What about the young girl who sat at home embroidering her wedding garments? Did she dutifully spend six hours a day sitting by the window in order to complete the required textiles for her trousseau?

One thing we know for sure is that the young woman who embroidered her wedding garments was not bothered by the urgency of the telephone, fax or e-mail, nor did she break off her constant repetitive motions to push the buttons on her remote control. She had long periods of concentration allowing intense focus on her work. The rhythm of her stitching created its own momentum and force. She had many demands to make of the completed garment. It had to represent her very best efforts because it reflected her qualities as a human being – her constancy, her talent, her dedication – and therefore it defined her position in the community.

That such time and effort should be devoted to a functional garment seems almost preposterous by today's standards. Even haute couture garments or the most elaborate evening gowns take only a fraction of the time and effort devoted to a Tai wedding dress. The fact that all the textiles in the Mises' possession were once worn makes their collection all the more richly deserving of preservation. Bold *ikat* robes from Uzbekistan, beaded skirts from Borneo, palm fibre jackets from the South Philippines, the silk garments of the Bogi-

Laos, from left to right:

Tai Nuea silk shawl (pha biang) *decorated with supplementary silk weft geometric designs.*
200 × 43 cm

Tai Phuan silk shawl (pha biang) *decorated with supplementary weft, showing horizontal colour effects and small geometric motifs.*
170 × 47 cm

Tai Daeng silk shawl (pha baeng) *decorated with silk supplementary weft, in geometric, palm and mystic diamond design.*
210 × 47 cm

nese people of Sulawesi – these garments are irreplaceable in today's world. Likewise, the techniques by which they were made are also rarely in use. Some garments were fashioned by cutting material and sewing the pieces together but many, such as the Balinese scarf intended to be wrapped around the body, are flat textiles. There are many ingenious ways to cover all or part of the body by wrapping it with a flat textile. Lengths of fabric can be simply thrown over the shoulders or slipped between the legs and wrapped around the waist, or sewn into a tube to serve as a cover from head to toe or any part thereof. The idea of cutting and shaping material to form a garment was a long time coming because it was a wasteful idea. It was better to weave the garment the necessary size both in length and in width.

Two examples of this in Asian costumes are part of the concept that so interests Marcel. The first is the small jacket from the Kauer people of Sumatra. The jacket is woven in one length with a solid blue panel through the centre and stripes on each side. After the textile was woven to the exact size required, it was cut into three sections. The largest section became the front and back with no shoulder seam, a typical feature of Asian garb. The centre blue panels were then decorated with embroidery to the point where the blue was barely visible. The other two sections were sewn to the centre to become sleeves. The unembroidered blue panel of the sleeves revealed its clever construction. The areas under the arms were not sewn, allowing ventilation in hot weather and creating less tension on the fabric. The second concept to fascinate Marcel is the one-size-fits-all method seen consistently in Asia. For a Japanese *kimono*, fabric is woven to a standard width and length, and adjustments for the size and shape of the individual wearer are made by folding the garment to fit. *Kimono* width is a standard form of measurement in Japan, just as a metre or yard in the West. The technique of shaping garments by cutting or sewing results in waste, in that parts of the labour-intensive fabric will be cut away and unused. For this reason, the cut-and-sew technique only became widely used when it became necessary to have clothing worn snugly against the body so that armour could be worn over it.

Collecting is a mixture of emotional responses and intellectual pursuits that come together to form a passion. When Zaira and Marcel discuss their connection with contemporary art, they talk about the astonishing way in which artists express themselves. Technique is irrelevant. They both express the sense of emotion they feel from the interaction with a work of art, though it may take some time with the material to understand the message, or the intent of the artist may not be clear and instead something expressed in the work reaches out and connects to their emotions in another way. No matter how it progresses, this interaction with the creativity of the artist is its own reward, Zaira says.

The Mises' experience with contemporary art is different from the possessive quality elicited by the costumes. The collecting of textiles for the Mises begins with the adventure of the search, the pleasure of finding a hidden treasure buried under the more known and desirable material at the flea market or discovering curious objects on a distant trip. What attracts the eye of Marcel is different from that which arrests Zaira's attention. She responds to what she terms the textile's "personality," meaning the image, composition, colour and perhaps an unusual quality she has not been aware of in other pieces. She responds to contemporary art in much the same way. Zaira's reaction remains a first impression based on aesthetics. Marcel, who says he must "penetrate a painting," steps in closer to examine the detail, technique and workmanship, even turning a garment inside out to understand its construction better. He is drawn to technical points such as the attention to a seam or the choice of a lining fabric. Each garment becomes its own adventure. A discovery of a small detail such as a hidden pocket offers a clue to its past usage. The continuous repeat of a minute *batik* design speaks to the energy of repetitive motion. Fine embroidery stitching in perfect rows communicates patience. Even signs of wear signify importance and love.

These costumes come from cultures where the makers did not sign their creations. This was not because they sought anonymity. In many cases, it was probably the opposite. They hoped that their peers would recognize the outstanding quality of their work. Without formal signature or sign, the identity of the maker is firmly embedded in the object, yet outsiders cannot discern it and this information rarely travels with the textile when it leaves its original home. But that does not mean that the textile remains anonymous. Most of these costumes form part of a tradition defined as "the process of handing down information, opinions, beliefs and customs by word of mouth or by example: transmission of knowledge … through successive generations without written instruction." When information or techniques are passed on orally or by observation, this does not mean that they do not change or evolve. They do but, as

Indonesia, Sulawesi, Toraja
Rice paste indigo-printed batik (sarita*)*
with shell, wheel, betel leaf and sun
motifs, hung as banners for festivities
or used by warriors to wrap their
helmets in.
500 × 25 cm

there is no "permanent" reference, changes are less noticeable. Living in a world where change is constantly necessary, the idea of no or slow change brings a sense of yearning. Objects that are part of this slow evolution give us a feeling of connectedness to something that is missing in our lives. In Indonesia, "the ancestors" are part of the present, both as benevolent and as malevolent spirits. There is no break from one generation to the next. Continuity is essential. This is how the Mises view costumes from Asia: an unbroken chain of designs and ideas passed down from one generation to the next and holding their power within. When collecting, what you acquire may not be a completely conscious decision. Why do your antennae come out in one area rather than another? The Mises' collection of contemporary art includes works by now-famous artists including Basquiat, Chia, Kiefer and Warhol. These early paintings were purchased when the artists were relatively unknown. Today, the collecting of costumes and textiles is in a similar infancy. A few people have assembled great collections in this area, but textiles as art have not yet caught the at-

tention of the mainstream. Partly this is because it is difficult to learn about textiles and costumes. There are not many books on the subject, and those that exist frequently concentrate on a specific locale rather than on the medium. Even those museums with great collections rarely allow many textiles on view. If you are interested in textiles, you must be attentive to exhibition schedules and ready to travel. Nevertheless collectors of costume and textiles possess an instinctual passionate feeling, a fervent quality that does not depend on the reassurance of others.

When collecting textiles, discovery is important. As Zaira and Marcel Mis begin searching for a new acquisition, they are full of anticipation. Then they discover something beautiful and they feel themselves touched by it. They study the costume and learn about the culture that produced it. They become the protectors and guardians of skilled craftsmen who deserve respect and recognition. Almost magically, their relationship with their collection grows until it becomes an important – and incalculably rewarding – part of their lives.

Japan
*Detail of Sanskrit sign from a pilgrim's coat (*haori*) written in* sumi *ink.*

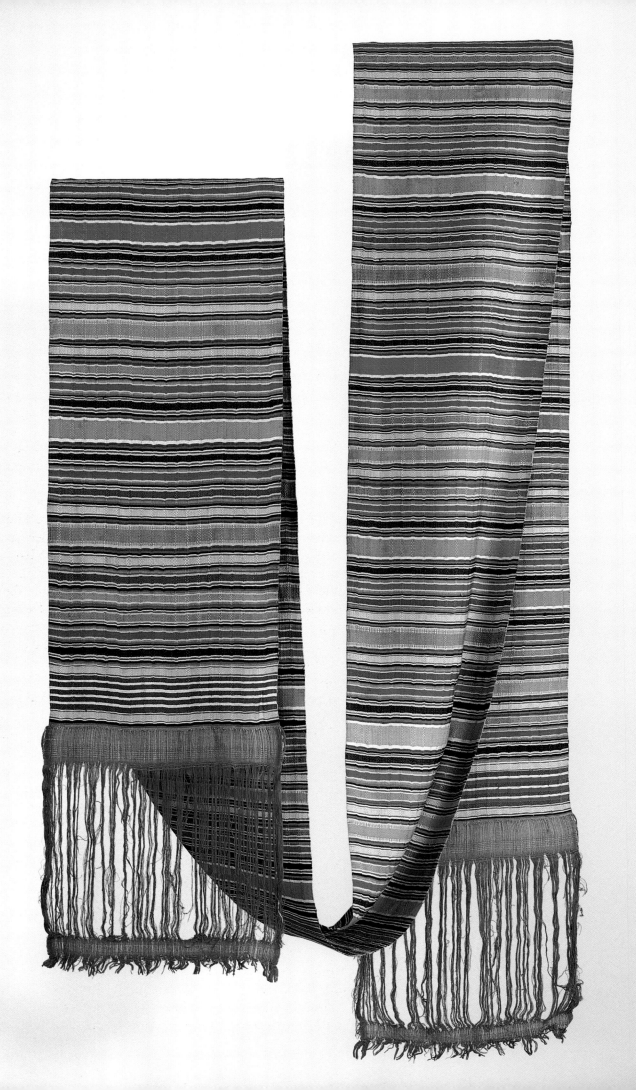

Frieda Sorber

Near and Middle East

The civilizations of the Near and Middle East have been renowned for their textiles since antiquity. The powerful empires of Persia provided an ideal setting for the production of luxurious fabrics destined to adorn emperors and courtiers. The trade routes between the Far East, Central Asia, the Middle East, the Mediterranean Basin and the West assured continuous links, both artistic and technological, which fertilized local textile production. Relatively little is known about the textile production of Persia and other areas in the Middle East. In antiquity many sculptures and bas-reliefs show magnificent costumes with elaborate designs. However, by the fifth and sixth centuries AD Sassanian silks were to be seen in the Byzantine Empire and far beyond. Silks and rugs found their way into church treasuries all over Europe, where many still survive after over a thousand years.

Between the fifth and the fifteenth century the Byzantine Empire provided a powerful base centred in Constantinople for workshops producing luxury silks, embroideries and costumes. For a long time the Byzantine Christians retained enough political and military power to maintain their own cultural traditions in the face of the influx of waves of invaders from Central Asia and the emergence of a new, rapidly expanding religion from the Arabian peninsula, Islam.

In the fifteenth century the Byzantine Empire finally gave way to a new world power. For centuries Ottoman Turkey would rule not only over its heartland Turkey, but over most of the Middle and Near East, North Africa and a sizeable part of Europe. The backbone of the empire was a well organized administrative and military network controlled by the Sultan. Istanbul became the centre where artistic elements from Central Asia, the Far East, Arabia, Byzantium and Southern Europe found a fertile ground enabling them to blend into a splendid material culture admired by many travellers, overawed by the richness and splendour of the Turkish way of life. In terms of dress the Ottoman Empire used the *kaftan*, originally a Persian garment, but probably also influenced by the costumes of Mamluk Egypt. The *kaftan* is a long outer garment with long sleeves, opening down the front and worn by both men and women. The most luxurious ones worn by the emperor and his court were made of sumptuous figured silks, many woven in the workshops of Istanbul and Bursa, but some of the them were made in Italian cities, especially in the fifteenth and sixteenth centuries. Turkish *kaftans* usually fastened in the front with small thread-covered buttons, each button the termination of a straight applied braid. In the eighteenth and nineteenth centuries braids and cords were applied in elaborate designs and were eagerly copied in many cultures. In Europe they found their way into military uniforms. In Moslem countries they would become a part of formal costume in areas extending from West and North Africa through Saudi Arabia and the Gulf States to India and even Indonesia.

Turkey also developed a unique and varied embroidery tradition. Male gold embroiderers at the Ottoman court in Istanbul were not only the direct heirs to the imperial Byzantine tradition, but they also absorbed influences from Southern and Central Europe, Persia and even the Far East. In the sixteenth and seventeenth centuries embroidery with gold and silver thread, embellished with precious stones and pearls, reached very high standards. In the eighteenth and nineteenth centuries

Ottoman Empire (Turkey)
Multicoloured fringed silk sash
(kuchak)
426 × 27 cm

23

Frieda Sorber

styles changed and European textile design influenced Turkish embroideries. European characteristics are also to be seen in the coloured silk embroideries on linen, silk and cotton. European-style flowers, landscapes and a general preoccupation with perspective influenced both Istanbul and other urban centres. The taste for pastel shades of silk, apparent in embroideries from the eighteenth and nineteenth centuries, has been linked directly to similar colour preferences in Western Europe in the eighteenth century. But Turkey also exerted an influence on Europe. The power of the Ottoman Empire in the sixteenth and seventeenth centuries was a very disturbing factor in European politics. By the end of the seventeenth century the domination of the Ottomans extended almost as far as Vienna, with Turkish rule firmly established in most of the Balkans. Towards the end of the seventeenth century diplomatic relations with the West intensified and many foreign ambassadors received Turkish costumes and *kaftans*, always presented in richly embroidered wrapping cloths (*bohça*). Much of what is now known of Turkish dress styles is derived from European eye-witness accounts, depictions by Western artists and artefacts looted from Turkish armies on the battlefields of Central Europe. Embroidery was omnipresent. It was used not only on clothing and wrapping cloths but also on divan covers, pillows, interiors of tents and even floor coverings. Gold embroidery on velvet and other silks was traditionally produced by male embroiderers, but silk embroidery, sometimes with added metal strips, was carried out by women. However, in addition to Ottoman officialdom, the Near and Middle East was the home for many other groups which often nurtured very different traditions, reflected in a diverse textile heritage. Persia never succumbed to the Turks and kept its own imperial traditions. In the West it is best known for rugs, which were used in Western interiors as early as the sixteenth century. But Persia also had a well-established silk, cotton and wool industry. Persian costumes made in elaborate figured silks, often bordered with bands from contrasting silks and lined with local printed cottons, show a high degree of refinement in cut. Wool tapestry woven costumes with *boteh* designs are closely related to the shawls of Kashmir in Northern India. Cotton fabrics printed with mordants and dyed red, pink, purple and black with madder reached Europe in the seventeenth century, where *toile perse* would become a household name for printed textiles.

But part of the wealth of the textile traditions lies far from the sophistication of urban centres. Both sedentary and nomad groups have developed their own costume and textile cultures, which have sometimes influenced the urban centres in their area. The *aba*, *abaya* or *bisht*, a rectangular coat in heavy wool worn by Bedouin shepherds, became standard male urban attire. In Saudi Arabia and the Gulf States, wool gave way to sheer cotton and the simple wool reinforcing stitches at the neckline and over the arms to elaborate gold embroidery. In Syria, Palestine and Egypt the *aba* became a stiff mantle woven in heavy silk and metal thread, draped over the head by both men and women.

Rural populations in Turkey, Palestine and Persia developed their own unique styles of clothing. Like courtiers and court officials all over the Near and the Middle East, their clothing styles were usually layered. Baggy trousers (or loincloths in most of the Arabian peninsula), vests, long-sleeved shirts and tunics or dresses were the components of many styles for both men and women. They were used in combination with small round hats, turbans or head veils. The fabrics were often locally spun, woven or embroidered. But some components, notably silk scarves, were made at a few urban centres and traded far and wide. So-called Aleppo scarves, usually in burgundy-coloured silk with beige or gold designs, found their way in both male and female costumes from South-Eastern Turkey to Palestine. Belts and scarves made by the twill tapestry technique best known from Kashmir and Persia were popular from Turkey to Southern Arabia and Egypt. The more expensive pieces came from India, but simpler versions were undoubtedly made locally.

Among the truly distinctive costumes of the Middle East are the ones worn by groups which are either geographically or culturally isolated. Only a few examples can be mentioned here. Yemen shares with neighbouring Oman a long tradition of indigo dyeing. A deep indigo blue is further deepened by the rubbing in of powdered indigo and vigorous beating. In both countries the indigo cloth was used for women's dresses, but elaborate embroidery is unique to Yemen. Religion divided the inhabitants of almost all the countries in the area. Jewish and Christian groups sometimes used the same costume as their Moslem neighbours, but more commonly costume was the outward sign of religious beliefs, as exemplified by the colourful embroidered silk dresses worn by Iranian followers of Zoroaster.

Ottoman Empire (Turkey)
Handkerchief (mendil yazma makrama) *printed black linen, with embroidered gold thread borders* (detail of p. 32).

Ottoman Empire (Turkey)
Dress (mecit entari) *in mauve and silver silk brocade with metal wrapped threads for needlework borders and plaited buttons.*
135 × 170 cm

Opposite page
Ottoman Empire (Turkey)

Sleeve detail of mecit entari.

Purse decorated with silver chain stitch Islamic embroidery edging, (oya).
22 × 15 cm

Leather slippers with sequins and silver embroidery.
25 × 7 cm

Ottoman Empire (Thrace or Albania)
Front and back of child's felt waistcoat with gold wrapped thread couched decorations, braids, trimmings, metal thread plaited buttons decorated with glass beads. Printed cotton lining.
35 × 35 cm

Ottoman Empire (Thrace)
Red silk velvet coat decorated with applications of corded gold embroideries and ribbons. Printed cotton lining.
110 × 240 cm

Ottoman Empire (Turkey)

*Vest in blue flannel with corded gold
and silk embroidery and red lining.*
60 × 150 cm

*Worn over a waistcoat in blue flannel
with corded gold and silk embroidery
and cotton lining.*
56 × 50 cm
Detail on opposite page

Ottoman Empire (Turkey)
Handkerchief (mendil yazma makrama) *in black linen printed and over-embroidered gold borders.*
72 × 50 cm

Opposite page
Ottoman Empire (Turkey)
Handkerchief (mendil yazma makrama) *in black linen printed and over-embroidered gold borders.*
54 × 43 cm

Ottoman Empire (Palestine)

Bedouin's headscarf (hatta) *in silk and silver brocade with silk tassels.*
142 × 120 cm

Kurdish silk and metal thread striped scarf with heavy silk and metal tassels.
136 × 150 cm

Opposite page
Ottoman Empire (Turkey)
Aydin. *Two striped silk scarves one with edges in diamond* (oya) *shape, the other with large floral and sequin* oya *decorations.*
90 × 84 cm and 136 × 64 cm

Ottoman Empire (Turkey)

*Cotton veil with tulip motif silk
embroidery on frontal part.*
160 × 75 cm

*Syria-tapestry-woven floral motif silk
cap.*
24 × 26 cm

Ottoman Empire (Turkey)

*Cotton veil with floral silk embroidery
on frontal part.*
161 × 78 cm

Purses in needle work "oya" technique.
12 × 8 cm

Opposite page
Ottoman Empire (Turkey)

*Linen towel (peskir) makrama
embroidered with metal strips and silk
threads in floral motifs.*
200 × 32 cm

*Pair of wooden clogs decorated with
mother-of-pearl applications.*
22 × 7 × 13 cm high

*Engraved turtle fan, gold-embroidered
with gold applications and sequins.*

Syria
Rural woman's cotton dress (thob) with
silk and tapestry embroideries.
124 × 122 cm

Opposite page
Palestine, Bethlehem
Cotton dress (thob), with embroidery
in silk and gold thread couching.
118 × 116 cm

Syria
Woman's cotton coat (yelek) with cross-stitch silk embroidery.
116 × 120 cm

Syria
Woman's cotton coat (yelek) with cross-stitch silk embroidery.
120 × 124 cm
Detail on opposite page.

Syria
Front and back of tapestry-weave tunic
(aba) in silk and metal thread. Floral,
striped and geometric design.
85 × 98 cm

Syria
Tapestry-weave royal tunic (aba) in silk and metal thread. Floral and striped motifs with silk lining.
90 × 100 cm

Iraq
*Front of coat (aba) tapestry weave with
blue silk and metal thread in geometric
and striped designs.*
130 × 142 cm

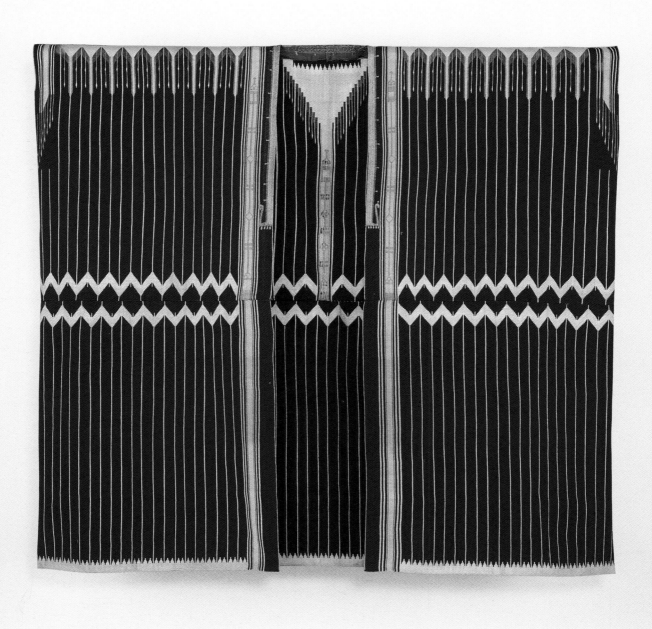

Iraq
Back of coat (aba) tapestry weave with
blue silk and metal thread in geometric
and striped designs.
130 × 142 cm

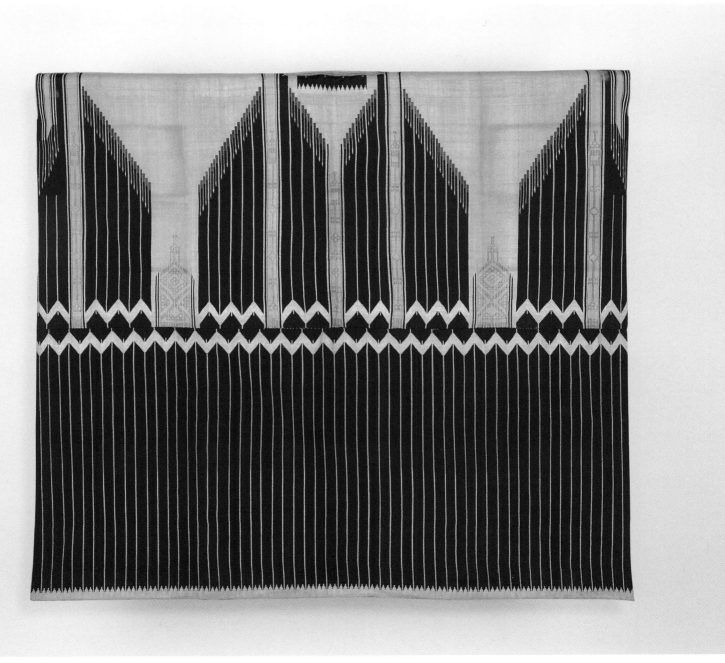

Syria, Aleppo
Front of imam's coat (aba) *in silk
and metal thread tapestry weave
and* appliquéd *corded gold embroidery
on yoke.*
132 × 114 cm
Opposite page: detail of the back

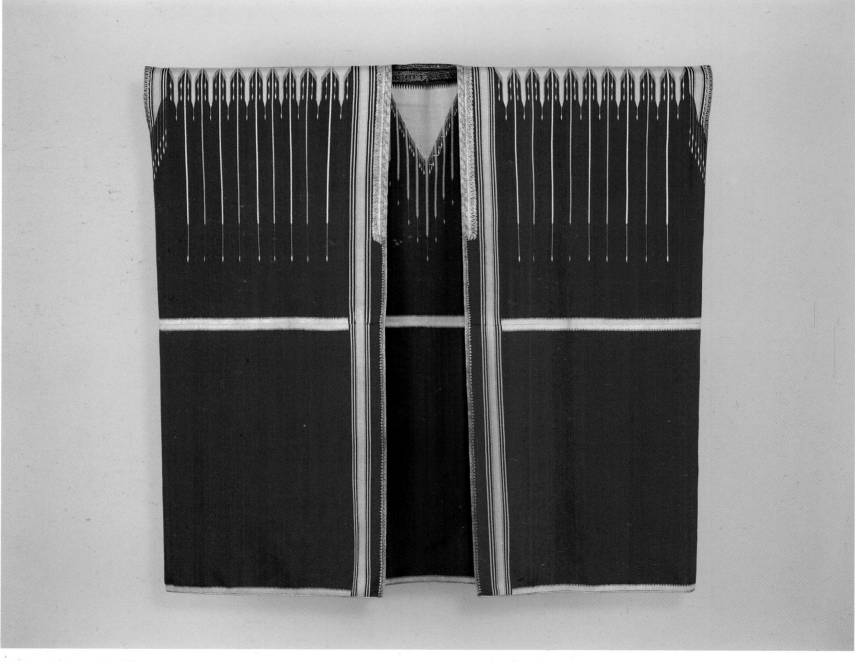

Syria
Double-faced coat in quilted satin silk.
115 × 125 cm

Iran, Jazd
Dress in printed Persian chintz with printed lining, quilted together and edged in blue cotton.
120 × 250 cm

Opposite page
Iran, Kirman

Embroidered woollen Dervish hat, with boteh *designs.*
30 × 14 cm

Wool shawl with brocaded boteh *designs.*
208 × 93 cm

Iran, Zoroastrian
Silk scarf with naïve *embroidered flowers and animal designs.*
280 × 83 cm
Detail of central part embroidery on opposite page

Iran, Zoroastrian
Red and green silk dress with small floral and animal silk embroideries.
116 × 125 cm
Opposite page: detail of embroidery

Yemen
*Shiny indigo blue cotton dress
embroidered with silk, copper and
mother-of-pearl elements.*
125 × 230 cm

Yemen
Dress in yellow silk striped reps, silk and metal embroidery with button applications.
122 × 220 cm

Yemen
Back of cotton dress with sequins and
metal thread embroidery, cotton lining.
102 × 151 cm
Detail of front embroidery
on opposite page

Valérie Berinstain

Central Asia

A land of contrasts, this part of the world comprises many countries with rich textile traditions. From the north of Iran to China, its arid land was inhabited by nomads who travelled with their herds from one pasture to another. They had to be able to pack all the items required for their daily life in bags or fabrics. Attractively coloured textiles and carpets with stylized floral designs were easy to carry and formed part of their environment.

All the fabrics made in this area are in silk and in cotton (*pakhta*), both of which are produced by the population. In what is now Uzbekistan, most families breed silkworms around wheat or cotton fields. This was done by the women, while the men boiled the cocoons in order to extract the silk thread. Before being woven, the thread was given to the dyers, who were often Jews. After having been dyed by the *ikat* tie-and-dye process, the thread was woven. Often the *ikat* fabric was composed of an ikated silk warp and a plain cotton weft. According to Islamic precepts it was preferable to have cotton in contact with the skin rather than silk, which was considered too sensual, but it seems that this precept was not applicable to women's clothes!

Most of the designs were in bright colours: pink, yellow, blue, red, green, violet and black, with large abstract motifs based on diagonal stripes or concentric circles imitating flowers. The fabrics were then cut in order to make upholstery, covers and also garments. The large centres of ikated textile manufacture were in the Ferghana valley. It was only with the arrival of ethnic groups such as the Turkomans, who were fleeing Soviet rule, that Afghanistan started producing silk and ikated silk fabrics.

Male Garments

Ikat garments in silk and cotton or in *ikat* or embroidered velvet were particularly sought after and were used by local royalty as a gift to their subordinates in pursuance of the Moslem practice of offering a robe of honour. Whilst ordinary men wore coats or *khalat* with multicoloured stripes, rich people did not hesitate to show themselves in many layers of *ikat* coats.

There are three types of *khalat*, all of which are long and open in front with sleeves covering the hands: the *yatak* is a thin mantle, the *chapan* is a padded coat for winter and the *chekman* is a sheepskin or camel-hair coat lined with cotton or silk. In all cases, the borders of the *khalat* are adorned with woven or embroidered braids (*sheyraz*). The *khalat* was worn over a long shirt and a pair of trousers. Very often, boots completed this attire. The most prestigious coats were those in cashmere wool velvet embroidered with gold or silver thread. They were synonymous with wealth and intended for the very rich. Some were made in the workshops of the great Khans such as the one in Bukhara.

Female Garments

The daily attire of the Turkoman and Uzbek women was made up of a pair of plain *ikat* or Benares silk trousers worn under a green or red dress, which was sometimes embroidered. This was covered by a coat, which could be in *ikat* or embroidered fabric and was sometimes adorned with coins or glass pearls. While nomadic women lived with unveiled faces, city dwellers were veiled. Their head was covered with a kind of coat with false sleeves. This coat-veil (*chyrpy*) was very often in cotton, embroidered with rows of stylized flowers, and among the Tekke its colour indicated the age of the wearer: blue was for

Afghanistan, Mangalli Nomads
Cotton woman's tunic with silk embroidery. The skirt is richly gathered at the waist.
(Detail of embroidery p. 63)

a young woman, yellow for a mature one and white for an old one.

These embroideries, the designs of which where mostly floral, were made by women.

Headgear

This is an important accessory used to permit identification of the ethnic group to which the wearer belonged. It can have four shapes: conical, following the shape of the skull, a simple cap or a four-sided cap.

These hats were always embroidered by women – who had the right to offer them for sale – with geometric designs, flowers, palms and lozenges. In general the threads used for embroidery came from cocoons which had holes and did not yield continuous threads.

All men wore, and still wear, a bonnet, which could be in silk or in embroidered cashmere. When outside, they covered this bonnet with a turban, the fabric of which indicated their social status. Those in white cotton imported from India were worn by the wealthiest.

Unmarried women, too, wore entirely embroidered bonnets to which jewels were attached and which were covered by a veil.

Whilst the garment was the pride of the various Central Asian peoples, upholstery also played an important part in their daily life. The best known are the *susani*, the wealth of whose floral designs is unequalled. These were made by women in cotton and embroidered in multicoloured silk thread to decorate their homes. This colourful upholstery, associated with the ornamental wealth of the garment, provided a contrast to the arid and monotonous environment.

Opposite page
Turkmenistan, Tekke
Embroidery detail of *chyrpy*
on page 68.

Opposite page
Turkistan, Pashtun
Cotton robe, back and front with embroideries, with 2 silk and cotton tassels decorated with beads.
118 × 120 cm

Afghanistan, Mangalli Nomads
Cotton woman's tunic with silk embroidery. The skirt is richly gathered on waist.
94 × 160 cm

Afghanistan, Turkmen
Woman's silk robe with cotton and silk embroidery. Cotton, metal, silk, bead decorated tassels.
110 × 170 cm
Opposite page: detail of tassels and hem embroidery

Afghanistan, Turkmen
Women's robe in cotton, silk velvet decoration on sleeves. Floral and geometrical embroidery decorations in silk and metal threads.
113 × 168 cm

Swat Indus-Kohistan
Women's cotton robe (jumlo) with cross stitch silk embroidery on front, sleeves and back. Decorated with glass beads, buttons, mother-of-pearl, coins, zip, plastic and metal items ; the full skirt has over 400 multiple inserted triangles.
90 × 146 cm

Opposite page
Swat Indus-Kohistan

Cotton child's head dress, with silk embroidery decorated with glass buttons, beads and coins.
62 × 54 cm

Cotton child's head dress, with silk embroidery decorated with glass buttons, beads and coins.
75 × 59 cm

Children's waist coat in cotton, decorated with silk cross stitch embroideries, glass beads, buttons, zip.
45 × 56 cm

Turkmenistan, Tekke
Married women's black silk mantle (chyrpy) pulled over the head when worn. Floral and shrub embroideries in cotton and silk, red and black fringes; the mantles of young women have black ground.
130 + fringes × 160 cm

Opposite page
Turkmenistan, Tekke
Married women's yellow silk mantle (chyrpy) pulled over the head when worn. Floral and shrub embroideries in cotton and silk, red and black fringes. The mantles of middle aged women are yellow.
116 + fringes × 58 cm

Uzbekistan, Bukhara
Mantle (kurta) silk warp ikat, silk borders; the lining is in imported printed cotton.
130 × 196 cm

Turkistan, Karakalpak people
Bridal head and face cover (kimishek), top is in felted wool, with cotton and silk embroideries and fine borders. Back part is in Bukhara warp ikat silk, fringes and tassels are in silk. This ritual head-dress was first worn when the bride moves to her groom's home.
160 × 168 cm

Uzbekistan, Bukhara
*Silk coat (*chapan*) with warp ikat,*
large circles and diamond designs, pink
borders and cotton lining.
143 × 190 cm

Uzbekistan, Bukhara
Dignitary's coat (khalat) *in Russian silk*
gold thread brocade, silk ikat lining.
133 × 162 cm

Uzbekistan, Bukhara
Silk woman's mantle (khurta). Two colours warp ikat, with tree of life motifs and silk borders; the lining is in printed cotton imported from Russia.
140 × 198 cm

Uzbekistan, Khiva
*Silk velvet coat of a dignitary (*chapan*),*
floral ikat motifs with embroidered
cuffs. Lining is in printed Russian
cotton.
123 × 178 cm

Uzbekistan, Bukhara
*Dignitary's coat (*khalat*) in silk velvet
and gold brocaded Russian fabric.
Woven borders. Silk ikat lining.*
135 × 200 cm
Detail of the back brocade motif
on opposite page

Uzbekistan
19ᵗʰ century Bokhara coat made for an Ottoman dignitary. The Chinese brocaded silk is embroidered in chain stitch silk thread forming the Nimuri *fruit motif; lining is in printed cotton fabric from Russia.*
144 × 173 cm
Opposite page: detail showing brocade, embroidery and tulip motif border

Valérie Berinstain

India

From the Ancient Origins of Cotton to the Silks of Bengal

India is a country of exciting and colourful fabrics. Everyone is familiar with the beauty of its multicoloured silks, but it is often forgotten that two of the oldest cotton plants, *Gossypium arboreum* and *Gossypium herbaceum*, originated there. Proof of the existence of cotton fabrics in the subcontinent as far back as about 1750 BC is provided by canvas fragments found at one of the most important sites of the Indus civilization, Mohenjo Daro.

For a long time one of the principal areas of production was Gujarat in north-west India. Besides being widely used by Indians, these fabrics were soon being exported to East Asia as well as to the Middle East and Europe. However, it is mainly from the seventeenth century onwards that cotton fabrics (chintz, gingham, etc.) became very well known in Europe.

While Indian cotton fabrics were popular in Europe, the silks were mainly used domestically. Contrary to general belief, the subcontinent has never been a large producer of silk, which was often imported from China and Persia. In fact, only the eastern regions produced – and still produce – a natural silk. This silk, rougher than bred silk, is called *muga, eri* or *tussah*, the most beautiful of these being *tussah*, produced in Assam in its natural gold colour. Silk garments are worn during ceremonies and banquets and are considered to be religiously pure, whereas cotton garments are used every day. The same distinction exists between sewn and non-sewn garments such as the *dhoti*, the *sari* and the *stoll* (*dupatta*), which are regarded as pure and can thus be worn during religious ceremonies.

Variety of Indian Costumes

Even if the general Indian population wears non-sewn garments such as the *dhoti, odhni, lungi, sari* or *dupatta*, princes and kings often wore garments with complex cuts.

Male costume

Except for the headwear, this is substantially the same for men of both the Hindu and the Moslem religions.

The poorest classes wear a *dhoti*, which is a piece of fabric placed around the hips and passing between the legs, or a *lungi*, which is a cloth knotted round the hips. Sometimes this modest wear is completed by a *kurta*, or skirt.

In contrast, the princely garments that have come down to us are incredibly sophisticated. In general, they are made up of a pair of trousers (*paijama*) and a tunic (*angarkha* or *jama*). The latter is most often worn for specific occasions.

The *angarkha* – from the Sanskrit *angrakshak*, which means protection of the body – may cover the bust or go down to the calf. Open at the front, it is made of cotton for daily use, while silk, velvet or wool are employed for wearing at ceremonial gatherings. It may also be embroidered. The *angarkha*, decorated with embroideries around the neck, on the shoulders and in the back, is known as *Farrukh sahi*, after a Mogul Emperor of the eighteenth century who was particularly fond of this type of ornamentation.

During important ceremonies, the *angarkha* is often replaced by the *jama*. This is made up of an upper part closed by braids on the side and a kind of skirt the length of which varies depending on the period. It can be made of cotton muslin or of any other precious fabric such as silk or velvet. It

81

is very often ornamented by very fine woven or embroidered motifs.

Upper class men often wear over their *angarkha* a *chuga*, which is a type of overcoat made of muslin for summer and of wool or quilted cotton for winter. The headwear is of great importance in the male Indian costume. All men, from the rajah to the villager, wear a turban or some sort of plain head cover.

In the nineteenth century the traditional turban was gradually replaced by the bonnet and hat in the large cities of India. As it became an ornament, the headwear saw many innovations. In northern India, the headgear worn by the middle classes became more and more extravagant.

One of the most interesting types of headwear is the *dolpari*, or beret, introduced to Lucknow by a prince from Delhi in the 1820s. This beret, decorated with gold or silver threads or sequins, much later and in a less ornate form became the emblem of the Indian nationalists.

Female costume

The *sari* is generally regarded as the symbol of India but from the sixteenth to the nineteenth century women mostly wore a skirt (*ghagra*) extending down to the ankles, a bodice (*choli*) or a blouse (*kurta*) and a veil (*odhni*).

The *ghagra* was in cotton or satin with flower or animal embroideries in silk thread, and sometimes with sequins, until the nineteenth century, after which Benares silk became the fashion. On important occasions, the skirt (*peshwaj* worn over trousers) was covered with gold or silver thread embroideries.

The skirt and bodice set was completed by a veil (*odhni*) which could be up to three metres long and two metres wide. One part was fixed to the belt of the skirt, while the other covered the head and fell over the back. The veils worn every day were usually in plain or ornamented cotton. For festivals or weddings the veil was in silk.

The women of Rajasthan still wear this costume today. In the far north, in the Punjab, the Himalayas, etc., the women prefer trousers (*salwar*) and the *kurta*.

The sari

This garment, which is now worn throughout India, was used mainly in the east and the south until the nineteenth century.

The *sari*, from the Sanskrit *sati* meaning a band of fabric, is mentioned in one the greatest epics of Hinduism, the Mahabharata (ninth century BC). Consisting of a long band of fabric draped around the waist and rising to the shoulder, the *sari* not only belongs to Indian tradition but its simplicity also symbolizes the grace of the Indian woman. In ancient times the *sari* was worn as a *dhoti*, and thus covered only the lower part of the body. It was not until the end of the eighteenth century that the modern *sari* appeared, combining the *dhoti* and the *stoll* (*dupatta*) in one garment.

The *sari*, about a metre and a half wide and over three metres long, can be draped in a variety of ways, depending on the region. Usually it is rolled and maintained over a petticoat, while the part over the blouse (*choli*) covering the chest is ornamented by a richly decorated band (*pallav*).

Each region of India has its own style of *sari*, which differs in fabric, weave, decoration and manner of draping.

Splendour and Diversity of Indian Textiles

Embroideries

The art of embroidery is principally dominant in the northern half of the subcontinent.

Despite the existence of court embroideries for the benefit of the princes and sovereigns of India, embroidery remains one of the great riches of Indian villages. Whilst the court embroiderers in the workshops of the capital cities (Cambay, Ahmadabad, Agra, Delhi, Lucknow, etc.) were men, village embroideries were – and still are – made by women, the art being handed down from mother to daughter.

The West

Gujarat has a reputation for embroidery. This region not only produced the most beautiful court embroideries but embroidery was present in the everyday life of the peasants and nomadic tribes. In this arid and poor region, decorative elements (*torana*, *chakla*, etc.) and garments are covered by multicoloured embroideries. From childhood, young girls are taught embroidery in order to prepare their wedding *trousseau*.

Female imagination as well as tradition leads to the creation of numerous geometric or very stylistic designs inspired by everyday village life. Animals, human forms, flowers and mythological elements intermingle and give rise to a great variety of decorative compositions. This abundant decor permits the identification of the social group to which the wearer belongs. This is particularly the case for the pastoral tribes of Sindh, Saurashtra and Kutch.

All these embroideries are made on thick cotton fabric with silk thread. Small mica discs reflecting light lend the textiles an expensive appearance.

The higher castes, often traders, usually use silk for embroidering skirt and blouse sets or superb dresses (*aba*) for their daughters' weddings.

The North

One of the main northern provinces is Kashmir, which has always been renowned for its woollen fabrics, including the famous shawls.

The oldest known specimens date from the end of the seventeenth century. They were then woven from wild goats' wool and the ornamentation was in flower designs inspired by Mogul art. In the nineteenth century shawls were covered by palm designs, which made their reputation in Europe. In view of the growing demand for shawls, Kashmir craftsmen sometimes replaced the woven design by an embroidered one as this took less time to make.

Among Punjab products *phulkari* (meaning floral art), including the *bagh* (garden), are textiles which up until the nineteen thirties were embroidered by women. These are large cotton veils made up of two or three breadths of thick fabric, often red, sometimes white, blue or brown and entirely decorated with floss silk yarn embroideries in orange, yellow, red and white. These designs are very stylized representations of such objects as the moon (*chandar phulkari*), ears of corn, peacocks (*mor phulkari*) or village scenes (*sainchi phulkari*), these last being the most rare.

Some *phulkari* were made by the grandmother for her granddaughter. At the time of the wedding, the young woman was wrapped in a *phulkari* by her maternal uncle. Eleven days after the birth of a son, the young woman covered herself in a *phulkari*. These veils were also used at funerals to place round the deceased.

The East

Bengal has a long and impressive tradition of embroidery and the most ancient examples of it are the pieces destined for the Portuguese in the sixteenth century.

The most refined of them, made in Dacca and Lucknow, are the *chikan kari*, which are feather, *buta* (palm) or flower designs in white or off-white, in the same colour as the muslin fabric. Sometimes sequins and scarab wings are added.

In addition to the above, until the nineteen fifties there used to be a farm production, known as *kantha*. The *kantha* is a cloth formed of many thicknesses of cotton fabric retrieved from old white cotton *saris*. Once they have been stitched together, the women decorate the *kantha* with a design which is symbolic (in that it is quincuncial) and also inspired by everyday life. These designs are embroidered in a great variety of designs with colour threads also retrieved from old *saris*. Thus, lotuses and soldiers, boats and life trees, elephants and trains are to be found together in houses, since *kanthas* are used in the family as bedcovers, bags, pillows, carpets, etc., some being donated to the temple.

Tie-dye decorations: ikat - bandhani - laharia

Among the extraordinary variety of Indian textile ornamentation, the tie-dye process is widely encountered in regions of Gujarat and Rajasthan as well as in Orissa and Andhra Pradesh.

The design is produced either by tying together the warp and/or weft threads before they are dyed so that it appears during weaving (*ikat*), or by tying together parts of a fabric before they are immersed in the dye (*bandhani* and *laharia*).

The Gujarati *patola* is one of the better known *ikat*. This silk *sari*, which is worn at important ceremonies, is made using the double *ikat* technique, i.e. with the warp and the weft threads both "ikated".

Historically, the first writings mentioning the existence of *patola* go back to the eleventh century. *Patolas* adorned with *treille* motifs with stylized hearts, flowers or elephants in red, yellow, green, blue or white tones have played a very important role in exchanges between India and Indonesia. These *patolas*, which are still very much in demand, are now woven only by some families in Paithan. *Bandhas* from Orissa are more rustic and are simple or double *ikat* fabrics in which yellow and red are dominant. Whether in cotton or in silk, the decor was originally geometric, and floral and figurative motifs came to be included from the beginning of the twentieth century.

In Andhra Pradesh, the *telia rumal* (which means "oily handkerchief", because they are oiled after dyeing) was and still is widely used as a *longhi* or as a turban by fishermen and the cattlemen of the Chirala area.

These squares, woven using the simple or double ikat process, are decorated with a red, white and black chessboard, animals (lions) or everyday objects (clock, aeroplane, etc.).

Gujarati and Rajasthan *bandhanis* have designs such as a large number of small circles (*bindhi*) placed according to a precise design, such as elephants, flowers or parrots, or geometric designs, these latter being preferred by Moslems.

The craftsman starts by folding the cloth in four and then sketches the designs with a reddish mud. Finally, with his nail, or a sharp point, he pushes

a cone of fabric and ties it with a knotted thread. The cloth is then plunged into the dye pot, only the tied parts not being dyed.

Most of the pieces kept in the collections are no earlier than the nineteenth century, but the wall frescoes of the Ajanta caves (fifth century) show some examples of *bandhanis*.

Still frequently worn by the women of the North West, veils decorated using the *bandhani* technique show a quincuncial design of five large circles.

The *laharia* (*lahar* means "wave") technique also involves the folding and tying of a piece of cloth before it is immersed in one or many dyes and is mainly used for decorating turbans. These turbans, over ten metres long and with a herringbone design on cotton muslin, were particularly in favour with the rajahs of Rajasthan.

Made-up silks

The most prestigious fabric for *saris* is *kinkhab*, or Benares brocade. This is woven out of brightly coloured silk and decorated in gold or silver threads with varied and complex designs (flowers, *buta*, animals among leaves).

From the fifteenth century onwards, Benares, or Varanasi, the sacred city of Hinduism, was reputed for its textile production but it was not until the nineteenth century that the first information about gold and silver thread (*zari*) decorated silks appeared.

The *sari* is usually decorated with a repetition of a small design (*buta*, or little flower), only one end, the *pallav*, which falls on the bust, being abundantly decorated.

Patahnis were also considered as particularly valuable *saris* and were included in the dowries of young women from Maharashtran high society.

They were made in Paithan or Aurangabad of silk with a border (*pallav*) consisting of a gold thread panel decorated with multicoloured thread representing parrots, geese, leaves and, most frequently, flowers. They were woven using a tapestry technique.

Bengal produced splendid *saris* such as *baluchar* and *jamdani*. The former were woven in silk in the village of Baluchar in Murshidabad district. Often the weft threads and the warp threads are in two different colours, but in all cases the reds, violets, yellows and beiges are quite dark.

Just like other *saris*, the *baluchar sari* is decorated with *buta*, or little flowers, but the *pallav* is, curiously, adorned with Western and Indian characters and with Western designs, such as boats, railway engines and trains.

Jamdani are made in cotton with an adornment based on foliated scrolls and *buta* in white and blue, sometimes highlighted with gold and silver threads. These textiles, which are mainly woven in Dacca, were at the end of the seventeenth century one of the tributes of Bengal to the Mogul Emperor Aurangzeb. One of the most beautiful *jamdani* was the one worn during the Diwali festival. As it was woven in dark blue with gold thread decorations, the woman who wore it disappeared into the night. Only the golden decoration shone, as did the lamps commemorating the event.

Conclusion

This brief survey of Indian textiles shows the wealth of the subcontinent in this area. Even if many of these productions have disappeared in the twentieth century, many efforts are being made to ensure their revival and to prevent these cultural treasures from being lost to posterity.

India, Bengal
Heavy silk wedding sari *woven in
diamond motifs; the end (pallav)
is decorated with gold supplementary
weft floral patterns.*
928 × 135 cm

India, Lucknow
*Silk muslin headscarf (*dupatta*)
decorated with silver thread floral
motifs.*
265 × 63 cm

India, Bengal
*Shawl (odhni) in cotton muslin
supplementary weft technique
(jamdani), with gold and cotton floral
motifs. The end is decorated with two
kalkas and a gold border.*
240 × 116 cm

*Bangalore face cover (sehra) worn by
men of royal families on their wedding
day, made of gold cords and tassels
decorated with sequins, coloured silk
and metal threads; gold strips with
jasmine flowers pearls and ruby
decorations.*
92 × 27 cm

India, Bengal
Two cotton muslin royal wedding saris woven with the jamdani *technique. Brocaded with gold-wrapped blue cotton thread in floral motifs. The* pallav *is decorated with two large* kalkas *in each corner.*
472 × 109 cm; 968 × 120 cm

Opposite page
India, Bengal
*Three cotton muslin saris decorated by the supplementary weft technique (*jamdani*) with gold floral motifs and embroidered borders.*
488 × 112 cm; 486 × 112 cm; 480 × 112 cm

India, Bengal, Lucknow
Jamdani *pattern royal tunic in brocaded cotton muslin with cotton and gold metal threads.*
98 × 175 cm

Page 92
India, Gujarat
Cotton sari *and shawl (*dupatta*), decorated with printed gold leaf flower motifs. The end piece (*pallav*) is woven from gold-wrapped thread.*
456 × 87 cm; 425 × 25 cm

Page 93
India, Rajasthan

Cotton muslin, tie-dyed men's turban pag *with wave motifs (*leheriya*), worn during monsoon season. This five-colour one is for festive occasions.*
680 × 17 cm

Cotton muslin, tie-dyed men's turban pag *with dot motifs (*bundi*), worn during monsoon season.*
525 × 15 cm

Cotton muslin, tie-dyed men's turban pag *with diagonal motif (*mothara*), worn during monsoon season.*
525 × 16 cm

India, Kashmir
Men's cotton waistcoat brocaded with silk and metal threads in palm motifs. Plaited gold threads are applied on the yoke. Gold buttons and striped satin silk lining.
51 × 42 cm

Back of waistcoat decorated with gold-plaited motifs and applications of gold thread embroideries. Small gold thread buttons and striped satin silk lining.
40 × 40 cm

Opposite page
Pakistan, Hyderabad
*Man's silk robe (*angrakho*), brocaded with gold-wrapped threads in diamond motifs and woven gold thread ribbons with floral motifs.*
105 × 160 cm

Man's silk trousers brocaded with gold thread.
99 × 80 cm

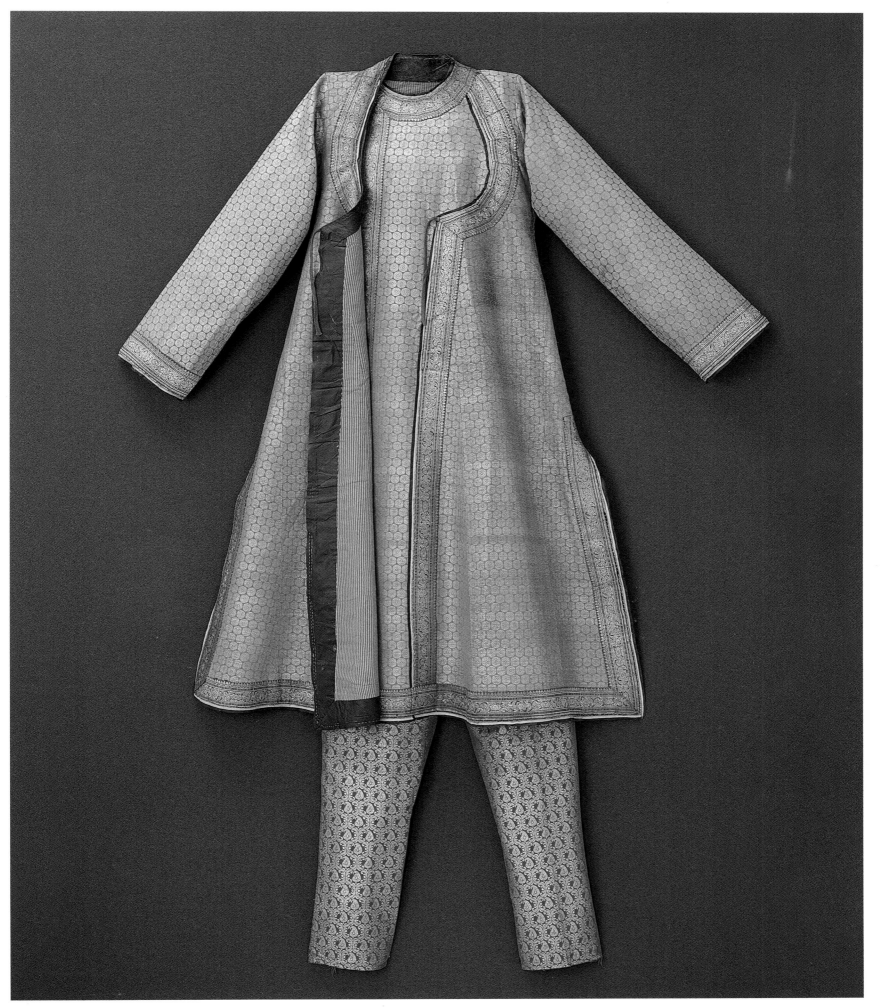

India, Kashmir
*Woollen men's coat (*chogha*), hand-embroidered and decorated in* jaal *pattern; front borders in* ambi *motifs; lining of white silk.*
125 × 180 cm

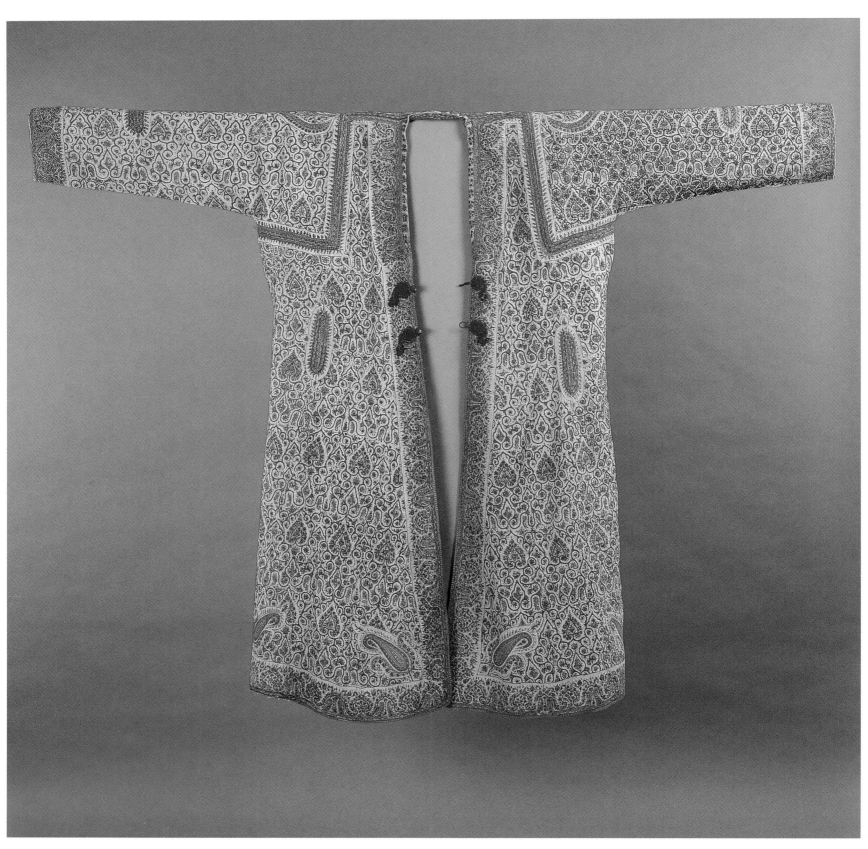

India, Kashmir
Black and red wool shawl (pashmina)
with applications of gold-plated metal
thread embroideries.
180 × 175 cm

India, Lucknow
Crown in gold, metal and silk threads, gold strips, sequins, floral decorations and fish motifs on top.
24 × 20 cm

India, Rajasthan
Man's wedding hat decorated with gold threads, pearls and sequins; edge covered with gold fringe.
22 × 17 cm

Opposite page
India, Kutch
*Woman's wedding robe (*khatri aba*) in* bandhani *satin silk decorated with metal ribbons and sequins; separately woven border.*
181 × 120 cm

India, Kutch, Gujarat
Headcover (odhni) in satin silk with bandhani *motifs; front border with silk and gold embroideries in tiny geometric designs and small mica mirrors.*
160 × 180 cm

Opposite page
India, Kutch Gujarat
Woman large satin silk dress (aba) worn over trousers (ezar) by merchant-class Moslems; minute silk embroidery with tiny mica mirrors and geometric designs; flat and loop stitches in flower motifs (banni).
115 × 140 cm

Opposite page
India, Kutch Gujarat
Woman wide satin silk trousers (ezar) worn under large aba. Tie-dye printed narrow cuffs have tiny geometric silk embroideries in flat and loop stitches, with small mica mirror decoration.
90 × 70 cm

Opposite page
India, Gujarat
Satin silk turban (gajji) printed with geometric motifs by bandhani *technique.*
952 × 78 cm

India, Kutch Gujarat
Silk shawl (odhni) in two panels with bandhani *embroidered with strips of gilded metal; one end-piece (border) has a woven band of gold-wrapped thread.*
146 × 180 cm

Opposite page
India, Gujarat
Double ikat *silk* sari *made by* patolu *technique; the centre is solid yellow, while the sides are decorated with double ikat flower and elephant motifs; borders are check-woven.*
360 × 137 cm

India, Gujarat
Double ikat *silk* sari *made by* patolu *technique with geometric and dancer designs in the centre and elephant, bird and flower designs in borders.*
360 × 132 cm

Opposite page
India, Gujarat
Double ikat *silk* sari *made by* patolu
*technique with elephant, flower, bird
and dancer designs in the centre.*
700 × 134 cm

Pakistan, Hyderabad

Double ikat *cotton* sari *(telia rumal)
with gold-thread embroidery.*
526 × 110 cm

*Simple and double ikated cotton shawl
(*telia rumal*) with geometric
gold-thread motifs.*
254 × 110 cm

Bangladesh, Dacca
Cotton sari *brocaded with multicoloured cotton threads in medallion and* bhoteh *motifs.*
370 × 90 cm

India, Baluchar Bengal
Brocaded silk sari *with dot motifs on the centre. The end piece* pallav *shows Indian and European figures in wagons (wheel-ships) and a large* kalka *in the middle. The centre is brocaded with dot motifs.*
440 × 116 cm

Opposite page
India, Benares
Silk shawl (odhni) *woven with gold thread and brocaded with peacock andparrot motifs; application of sequin borders.*
250 × 174 cm

Opposite page
India, Benares
Silk sari *brocaded with gold* bhoteh *motifs, small in the centre and large on the* pallav.
442 ×113 cm

India, Gujarat
Gold-thread brocaded silk sari *has a red centre with a gold coin pattern; the* pallav *and the borders are in gold-wrapped thread with lion, bird and flower motifs, in Paisley pattern.*
400 × 126 cm

India, Metiabruz
*Ceremonial silk skirt (*gaghra*)*
decorated with silver and gold-thread
embroideries and metal applications.
135 × 325 cm

India, Metiabruz
*Ceremonial silk skirt (*gaghra*)*

India, Bharatpur

Gold-thread brocaded royal silk skirt (gaghra) with bird, duck, deer, lion, elephant, horse, cow, tiger, peacock, camel and flower motifs. Thirty-four triangular panels have been woven and reduced at the waist to make a large sun-shaped skirt. Late nineteenth century.

This skirt was first woven for the princess of Faridkot, using seventy-three metres of fabric. One half was used for the wedding of her daughter, the Maharani Deergh of Nabha. It was subsequently split in two for the weddings of the Maharani's two daughters, and split up into more pieces afterwards.
95 × 612 cm

Pakistan, Sindh Dadu
Woman's silk tunic (chola) in different fabrics and colours, with silk embroidery, mirrors and gold-wrapped thread decorations.
99 × 148 cm
Opposite page: detail of embroidery

Pakistan, Sindh Lohana
Woman's silk wedding tunic (chola) in different fabrics and colours. Silk and metal thread embroideries and mirror (sisha) decorations and applications.
90 × 145 cm

Opposite page
India, Karnataka, Banjara
Backless blouse (kachali) decorated with applications, buttons, mirror ornaments and embroideries.
40 × 65 cm

Opposite page
India, Kutch Gujarat
Wedding blouse (choli) silk and cotton embroidery and applications with buttons and mirror ornaments.
54 × 140 cm

India, Kutch
Uncut skirt cloth (gaghra) *in satin silk with diamond and flower motifs in silk thread.*
73 × 480 cm

Opposite page
India, Kutch
Satin silk skirt (gaghra) *showing silk chain stitch embroidery with peacock and flower motifs.*
97 × 190 cm

India, Gujarat Budj
Woman leather and cotton slippers with chain-stitch flower motif silk embroideries (mocchi).
24 × 8 cm

Opposite page
India, Rajasthan
*Woman's headcloth (*odhni*) in wool
with geometric cotton embroideries.*
200 × 100 cm

India, Kutch Gujarat
*Young boy's cotton smock with silk and
cotton flower and animal embroideries.*
55 × 110 cm

*Cotton and silk headcover with flower
and animal embroideries.*
26 × 17 cm

India, Kutch Gujarat
*Young boy's cotton smock with silk and
cotton flower and animal embroideries.*

Pakistan, Sindh Kutch
Man's cotton wedding shawl (doshalo)
decorated by bandhani *tie-dye*
technique, silk embroideries and
applied mica mirrors.
226 × 127 cm

Opposite page
India, Banjara
Woman's cotton dress with folk
embroidery, applications of different
colours of fabric; skirt printed
and finished with border.
120 × 70 cm

Opposite page
India, Banjara
Embroidered purse and mirror,
decorated with coloured glass
and leather bead tassels.
19 × 6 cm

Pakistan, Sindh Kutch
Man's cotton wedding shawl (doshalo)

Pakistan, Swat
*Woman's cotton shawl (*chadar*) with floss silk embroidery and medallion motifs.*
252 × 135 cm

Opposite page
India, Tarbella
*Married woman's cotton tunic (*kurta*) with floss silk embroideries forming medallion designs; application of gold thread embroideries around neck and fine silk embroidery on shoulders.*
89 × 158 cm

Pakistan, Swat, Lahore
Striped silk shalwar *with belt.*
105 × 75 cm

India, Sindh
*Woman's leather shoes (*taurauwari jaoti*) with wool tufts.*
25 × 10 cm

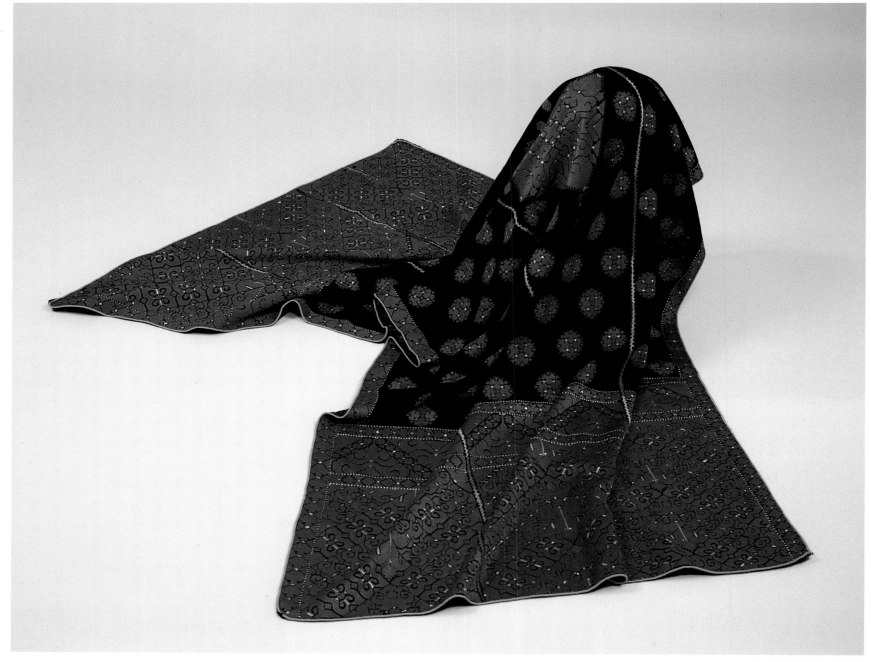

Pakistan, Swat
*Woman's cotton shawl (*chadar*) with floss silk embroidery and medallion motifs.*

Opposite page
Pakistan, Sindh, Hyderabad
*Children dress (*angrakho*) embroidered with floss silk yarn.*
62.5 × 65 cm

India
Children brocaded satin silk trousers with brocaded gold borders.
63 × 43 cm

Pakistan, Sindh, Hyderabad
Silk child dress with floral silk embroideries.
61 × 75 cm

Page 128
India, Punjab
Cotton sainchi phulkari *shawl embroidered with floss silk showing Indian daily life, children playing, trains and all the animals of India; borders with geometric motifs.*
218 × 122 cm

Page 129
Detail of embroider

Mary Hunt Kahlenberg

South-East Asia

Textiles in South-East Asia are symbolically female, their male counterpart being metalwork. This complementary relationship reflects the idea of unity as a combination of masculine and feminine elements. The process of weaving represents creation as a whole and human birth in particular. In many areas of South and South-East Asia, the loom and the weaver become one in a continuous re-enactment of the birth process. The weaver sits on the ground or floor with her legs stretched out in front of her. Her feet are placed against a bar, and her back is pressed against a back strap bar. Extending her body in this manner, she controls the tension of the warp threads. As she inserts the weft between the warp, the threads merge to become cloth. The advancing woven textile appears to come forth from her womb. (Dhamija, Jasleen, *Woven Incarnations*, paper given at the Textile Society of America Symposium 2000, Santa Fe, New Mexico)

South-East Asia is a broad geographic area but one whose history and origins have been closely connected. In the Mis collection, the area covered stretches from the Philippines across the chain of Indonesian islands to the mainland and north to Burma (modern Myanmar). Like the weaving process of taut warp and interlocking weft, the textiles and garments of this area have a strong, constant line that makes them recognizable as a group and yet sufficiently distinct so that one is able to identify an area of origin or even pinpoint an exact location. Over the years, regional populations were controlled by strong central governments, sometimes for hundreds of years, but as the power of these governments waned, this ethnic group re-emerged with much of its traditions intact. Viewing the area's costumes together as in this collec-

tion reveals how a diversity of outside influences were absorbed one after the other while strong community traditions provided the continuity for distinctive local styles and symbolism.

South and South-East Asian populations were formed by several waves of migrations. Traders from China, the Arab World, India and Europe brought their goods to be exchanged for the agricultural and mineral wealth of South-East Asia. All of these people contributed to the layering of beliefs that still define the peoples of South-East Asia. The original inhabitants of South-East Asia migrated from what was then mainland South-East Asia to Australia over 40,000 years ago. These peoples were hunters and gatherers using simple stone tools and without the accoutrements of settled life, such as pottery and textiles. The first peoples had a reverence for their ancestors because the continuity of their line was continuously in jeopardy, and this reverence for those who lived before was the beginning of a strong continuum of beliefs. Their shamans divided deities into the two categories that still continue today: male gods – related to the sky represented by birds – and female earth gods – represented by snakes. The Australian Aborigines, the peoples of the Indonesian island of Irian Jaya and Papua New Guinea, the Orang Asli or "original people" of Malaysia and southern Thailand and small groups in the Philippines are the direct descents of these peoples.

The second wave of migration from India and Burma by the Proto-Malays in approximately 5000 BC introduced the domestication of rice. This knowledge gave the newcomers immediate superiority over the existing populace. They, too, have kept their identity as a group and are represented in the Mis collection by the spirit-filled *ikat* textiles of the

Indonesia, Bali
Breast or shoulder cloth for women
(slendang) *with silk and metallic yarn*
brocade and fine weft ikat.
262 × 38.5 cm

131

Dayaks of Sarawak and the meticulously embroidered costumes of the Philippine Bagobo. The Deutero-Malays followed in another wave from southern China between 3000 and 1000 BC, travelling by sea along the Indochinese coast to Malaysia via the chain of islands now known as the Philippines and Indonesia. Sometimes the Proto-Malay and Deutero-Malay are grouped together and called Austronesians. Both groups settled throughout South-East Asia and with their knowledge of pottery and slash-and-burn rice cultivation, they also came to dominate over their predecessors.

By the end of 1000 BC, traders began exchanging Chinese finished goods for local Indonesian agricultural products. The Chinese objects, which included many bronze weapons, exhibited the rich decorative style that had already flourished for thousands of years in China. Curvilinear and spiralling forms, with their origins in the tendrils of plants, were transplanted into the fantastically stylized animal motifs of the densely designed Iban textiles and beadwork of Borneo.

South-East Asia changed substantially when India's influence brought irrigation in the first century AD. Surpluses of food provided the wealth for the elaborate religious and state structures also imported from India. In Hindu and Buddhist worldviews, states were patterned on the order of the cosmos and cosmological and magical symbols expressed this power. (Hall, Kenneth R., *Maritime Trade and State Development in Early Southeast Asia*, Honolulu, University of Hawaii Press, 1985, p. 6) What developed at this time was a mosaic of ideas, a blending of existing beliefs going back to the Orang Asli combined with a mix of Hinduism and Buddhism from India. This patchwork of religions covered the rich river valleys of Burma, Cambodia, Thailand, eastern Borneo, the Malay Peninsula and the Indonesian islands of Sumatra, Java and Bali. In these new religions, the king was at the top of the power pyramid because he claimed descendency from the gods. With the king's claim came the responsibility to ensure the benevolence of nature and the good health of the population. Hindu and Buddhist beliefs reinforced royal rights and responsibilities. Added to this was a symbolic relationship with perceived animal ancestors, among them crocodiles, elephants and birds as carriers of the spirits and souls that had dominated mythology for centuries.

The blending of Indic and indigenous traditions is seen throughout South-East Asia in the pyramid form of the mountain. The mountain had always been the sacred home of the ancestor spirits. In the Indian Hindu philosophy adopted by the area's rulers, the god Siva was "Lord of the Mountain"

for his association with fertility. (*Ibid.*, p. 5) By bringing these two related concepts of the mountain together – ancestor worship and fertility – the rulers enhanced their power and as a result, there was continuity in traditional ways and beliefs.

From these hierarchical systems, two major factors influenced textile design for garments. First, symbols of the spirit world that identified the owner/wearer's social position evolved from earlier shamanistic roles to representations of political power. The power of animals such as the dragon or crocodile was attributed to the rulers. Second, a new form of presentation arose which was based on the Indian aesthetic of stylized patterns of flora and fauna. This sense of pattern evolved over the years with amazing continuity. Motifs carved on the costumes of the statues of the ninth-century Javanese Buddhist temple Borobodur remain now in batik patterns associated with the courts of Central Java. Another persistent legacy was the sumptuous Indian textile tradition of brightly coloured silks brocaded with gold and silver threads. This can still be seen in the Mis collection in the brilliant fabrics from Malaysia, Thailand, Laos, Cambodia, East, West and South Sumatra and Bali.

In the eleventh century, Islamic traders traversed the straits of Malacca, a narrow opening between Malaysia and the Indonesian island of Sumatra, to trade in spices and to make contact with Chinese traders coming west. But it was not until the fourteenth century that Islam began to be adopted by local populations. Over the next few hundred years, Islam spread to the Malaysian Peninsula, parts of Sumatra and Java, the coastal areas of Sulawesi and to the Moluccas. In the converted regions, ceremonies changed to emphasize rites of passage rather than the previously dominant mortuary rites. The functions of some textiles were altered, and aesthetics and composition adapted to this new role. Animal and bird imagery lessened while floral and fauna designs continued in more abstract form.

When the Europeans, beginning with the Portuguese and followed by the English and Dutch, came seeking spices in the sixteenth and seventeenth centuries, they brought patterned, dyed textiles from India, continuing an already established exchange begun by Indian and Arab traders. This constant supply of imported goods must have taken its toll on local textile production, but how extensively is now difficult to judge. Trade records show that these patterned textiles were an essential part of the spice trade equation, and that textiles acquired for export in Indonesia were most frequently plain, woven, undyed goods. An important lost thread of knowledge is what designs were brought from India and how they influenced local aesthetics, as well as what adaptations were made in India specifically for the taste of Eastern markets, particularly those of Thailand, Malaysia, Sumatra, Java and Sulawesi. Fashion preferences established during this time have continued to the present day.

The importance of honouring ancestors was both an overriding force and a stabilizing factor that resulted in distinctive local styles with unique symbolism. While migrations and trade constantly brought new ideas, they were adapted into a specific aesthetic perspective. A slow metamorphosis of designs was both allowed and constrained by the close ties between these complexly designed textiles and the local religion. Because the designs of these textiles are tacit rather than explicit or literal, they form an emblematic language that represents a well-ordered and clearly understood social hierarchy that can only be truly deciphered by those educated into it. This means not only becoming part of the social structure but existing at the top of the social or religious hierarchy.

The use of one motif over another, such as the row of four large shrimp viewed from above in the man's *hinggi*, or shoulder cloth (page 202), from the island of Sumba in Indonesia, form a strong visual pattern accented by dominant characteristics of extended antennae and elongated bodies ending in wide tails. The realistic motifs of Sumbanese textiles and the powerful manner in which they are graphically combined have long made them popular with Westerners. Most of the creators they portray, however, are parts of complex metaphors that separate the initiated from the outside. These metaphorical equivalents used in ceremonies and woven into textiles constitute a Sumbanese visual vocabulary. It is usually at this metaphorical point that we as outsiders begin our understanding of these textiles. In this Sumba *hinggi*, the appearance of the shrimp motif indicates that its primary function is for burial.

In Sumbanese society, textiles serve as both a physical and a metaphorical protection against the uncontrollable cosmic forces that the soul may encounter while travelling from this world to the beyond. (Adams, Marie Jeanne, *Systems and Meaning in East Sumba Textile Design: A Study of Traditional Indonesian Art*, New Haven, Southeast Asian Cultural Studies Report Series 16, Yale University, 1969, p. 167) The shrimp is an apt symbol of this dangerous passage because it sheds its protective covering and is under threat while the new shell is growing in. This textile was produced for a ritual of a highly structured society where only royalty would be able to command this onward protection.

They were the only ones who possessed both the right to use this motif and the economic resources and time to produce a textile with this elaborate design. Knowing that the deceased was thus protected brought relief to those remaining. Learning the premise of this concept gives insight into the power of the textile. Increased understanding of its cultural context brings a greater respect and understanding of its power.

As the Bagobo or Meo or Iban weaver sat at her loom creating a textile from the weaving of warp and weft threads, she was also aware that she was an important part of her community and a link in a historical chain of textile weavers. She implicitly understood the larger picture of how her particular efforts were a representation of the idea of unity as a combination of male and female efforts and that her resulting garment would symbolize creation. Although similar beliefs are shared by many of the peoples throughout South-East Asia, distinctive local styles and symbolism have developed from strong community traditions. It is not unusual to be able to determine which village a particular textile comes from, or more often which clan or family produced and wore it, because the identity held within these costumes has remained strong for centuries. The information that each garment contains and the feelings that the costumes bring forth has for centuries given them the most prominent position of all material possessions. This collection begins to show us the depth and importance of social and religious context of Asian costumes and will enrich our view of dress throughout history.

Burma, Chin
Tightly woven cotton tunic with supplementary weft in geometric motifs; decorations with cowries and red glass beads. Worn by men and women; the brighter ones are women's.
49 × 51 cm

Burma, Kashin
*Woman's skirt (*pukhang*) in cotton warp and wool weft made in three parts; supplementary weft and silk thread embroidery decorations.*
145 × 83 cm

Burma, Kashin
*Woman's skirt (*pukhang*) and leggings, in cotton warp and wool weft; supplementary weft decoration in geometrical motifs.*
153 × 66.5 cm and 24 × 15 cm

Burma, Haka Chin

Cotton vest with supplementary weft in geometrical motifs. The front part is decorated with cowries, shells and grain fringes.
40 × 42 cm

Tube skirt with supplementary silk weft geometrical motifs.
138 × 86 cm

Burma, Haka Chin

Cotton vest with supplementary silk weft geometrical decorations and strings finished with grains. Tube skirt with supplementary silk weft decorations.
45 × 50 cm; 125 × 85 cm

Burma, Chin
Cotton tunic with silk and cotton supplementary weft in geometrical motifs. Silk diamond motif embroideries, beads and buttons decorate the front part.
52 × 62 cm

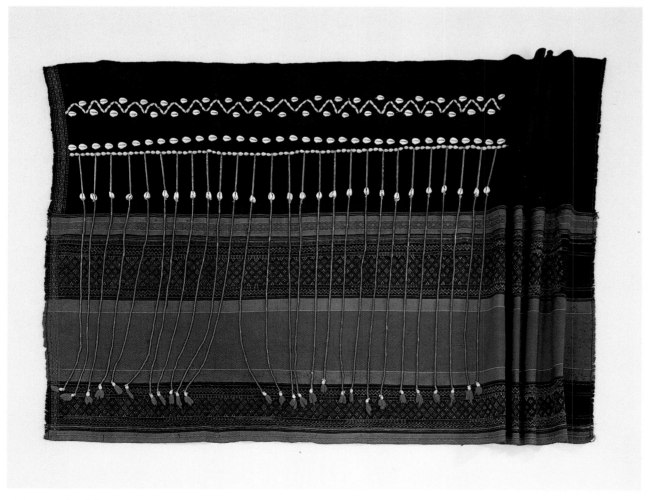

Burma, Haka Chin
Cotton tube skirt with supplementary silk weft and application of beads and cowry shells; hanging beads cowry shells and grains.
145 × 80 cm

Burma, Arakan state
*Three Khami people cotton breastcloths
(ad khin) with supplementary silk weft
geometrical motifs; ties in corners and
some silk embroidered motifs.*
125 × 34 cm; 77 × 37 cm; 75 × 32 cm

Burma, Yaw
*Tube skirt (longyi) with supplementary
silk weft in geometric patterns.*
115 × 85 cm

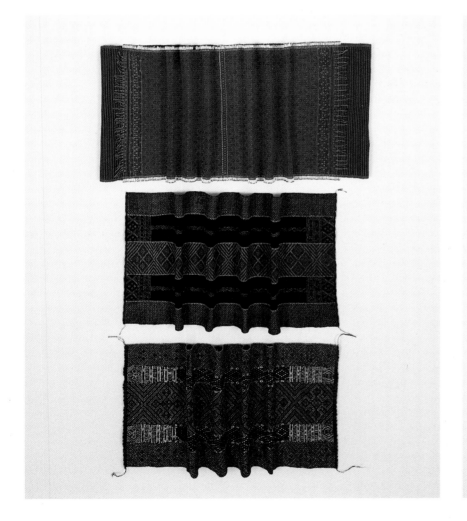

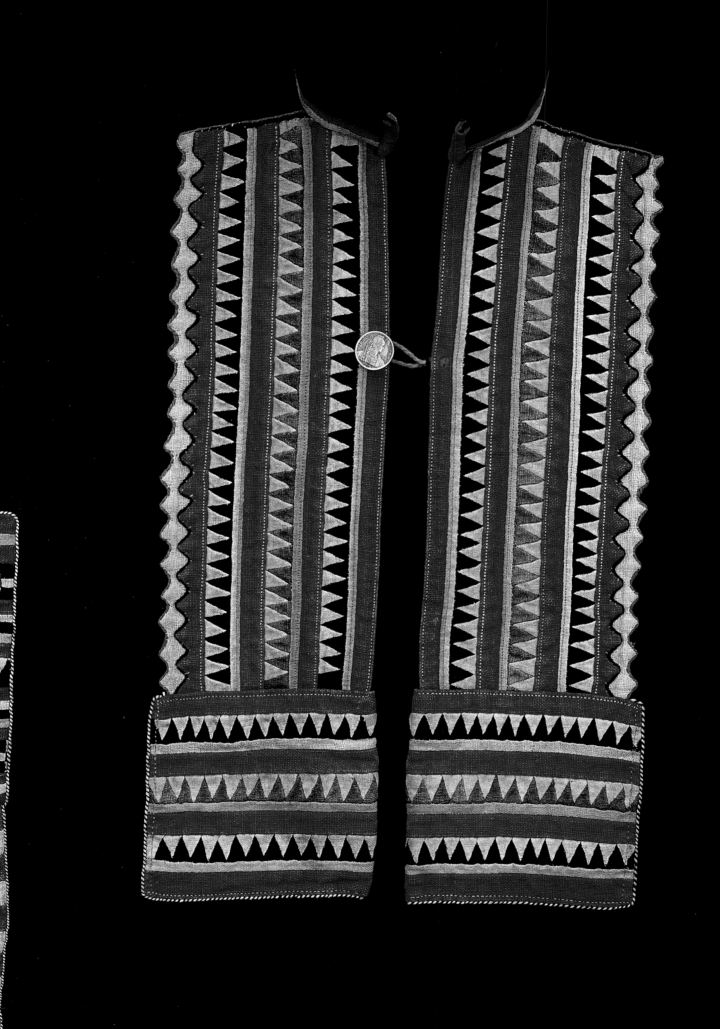

Burma, Lahu, Shan state
Cotton coat, can be worn by men or women. Appliquéd *pieces of cotton fabrics on yoke and sides with striping on sleeves.*
116 × 150cm
Opposite page: detail of front yoke

Opposite page
Thailand
Indigo-blue cotton bride's turban with supplementary weft geometrical motifs and hanging heavy pom-poms.
389 × 48 cm

Thailand, Lawa

Women's costume. Cotton blouse with silk and metallic embroidery on front yoke.
63 × 75 cm

Silk and cotton sarong *with warp* ikat *stripe design.*
75 × 52 cm

Thailand, Akha
Woman's cotton jacket with multicoloured cotton strips, appliqué patterns and couched threads on sleeves and back. Long bead and seed fringes hanging from the back.
65 × 160 cm

Thailand, Karen/Sgaw
*Cotton tunic worn by women on
wedding occasions, decorated with
appliqué cotton and vegetable seeds.*
79 × 72 cm

Opposite page
Laos, Tai Nuea
Pha biang *shawl made of cotton and silk by* khit *and* chok *techniques. Supplementary weft patterns showing abstract designs of mythical animals, diamonds and geometric designs. Long coloured silk fringes.*
200 × 42 cm

From left to right:
North Laos, Tai Nuea
Cotton and silk sarong (pha sin). *Supplementary weft patterns of abstract designs, diamonds, geometric figures.*
90 × 60.5 cm

Laos, Tai Nuea
Pha biang *shawl made of cotton and silk by* khit *and* chok *techniques. Supplementary weft patterns showing abstract designs of mythical animals, diamonds and geometric designs. Long coloured silk fringes.*
200 × 42 cm

Pha sin sarong *with alternations of weft* ikat *and supplementary weft used to dress wealthy deceased women.*
80 × 50 cm

Laos, Pha Chet
Tai Lue Muang Ngoen *from Nan province. Coloured cotton scarf worn by men on one shoulder. Continuous and discontinuous silk and cotton supplementary weft in geometric patterns. Silk pom-poms.*
124 × 30 cm and 160 × 30 cm

Opposite page
Laos, Tai Phuan
Long silk shawl (pha biang) for funeral offerings. With supplementary silk weft decorations showing human and animal designs.
716 × 43 cm

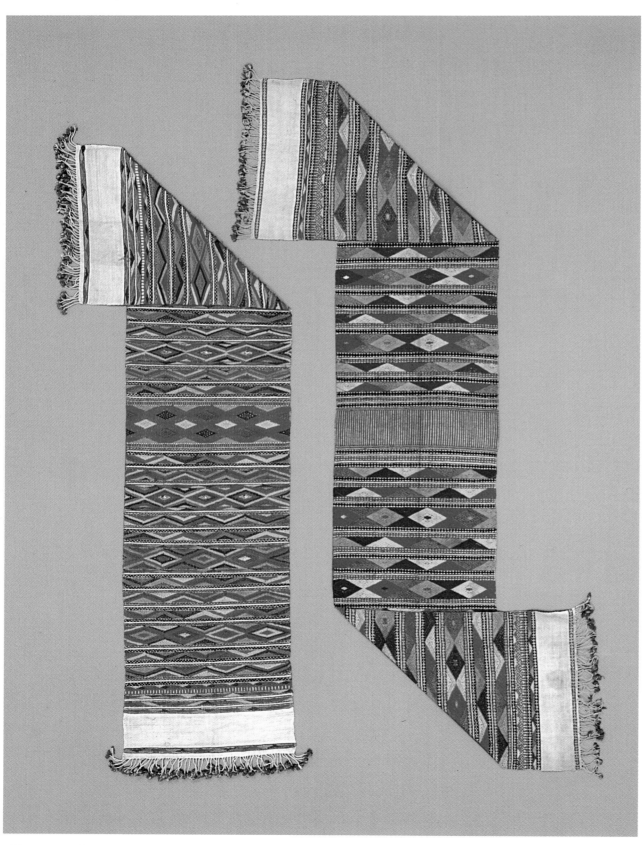

Cambodia, Pidan
Silk sarong *woven in three colours supplementary weft in small diamond motif and stripes*
300 x 85 cm

Large cotton and silk royal sarong *with very tight supplementary weft*
286 × 95 cm

Cambodia, Pidan
Silk sarong *weft* ikat *with ducks, dogs, peacocks and geometrical motifs.*
348 × 92 cm

Opposite page
Cambodia, Pidan
Silk sarong *weft* ikat *with geometrical designs.*
276 × 85 cm

Silk sarong *weft* ikat *with hens and geometrical wave design.*
369 × 87 cm

Philippines, Mindanao, Bagobo
Complete men's costume in vegetable fibre; the jacket and trousers are decorated with discs of mother-of-pearl, sequins and embroidery. Ground is ikat. The abaca fibre bag is embroidered with beads. The beaded belt has brass pendants. The other one has brass plates and pendants. The scarf, printed with a tie-dye pattern, has beads and cotton tufts.

Opposite page
Philippines, Mindanao
Kalagan abaca fibre blouse, reserve dye technique.
44 × 150 cm

Philippines, Mindanao
*Bagobo trousers (*blaan sawal*), ikat dye vegetable fibre embroidered with multicoloured cotton thread and mother-of-pearl discs decoration.*
48 × 44 cm

Philippines, Mindanao, Bilaan people
Kalagan abaca fibre jacket decorated with cotton embroideries showing geometrical and human motifs.
51 × 46 cm
Opposite page: detail of embroidery

Opposite page
Philippines, Ddgon, Kulaman people
*Cotton blouse (*umpak*), covered with*
*close circles of mother-of-pearl (*kalati*)*
giving magical protection.
39 × 41 cm

Philippines, Mindanao, Bagobo
Cotton blouse covered all over with
*mother-of-pearl discs (*kalati*) and*
coloured glass beads; fringes with brass
pendants.
50 × 42 cm

Bottom
Detail of mother-of-pearl disc
applications.

Philippines, Luzon, Gaddang
Paracelis. Man's cape in cotton stripe decorated with beads and embroidery.
120 × 89 cm

Silk headscarf, decorated with sewn glass beads.
60 × 57 cm

Opposite page
Philippines, Sulu
Silk skirt in three panels attached together with bands woven by tapestry technique.
164 × 93 cm

Opposite page
Philippines, Sulu Tansung
Long silk scarf, four-coloured tapestry weave technique.
282 × 32.5 cm

Opposite page
Indonesia, Kalimantan,
Dayak Maloh people

*Women's skirt in cotton with applied
beadwork and* nussa *shells. Worn
by members of the highest classes.*
46 × 42 cm

*Women's cotton ceremonial skirt (*kain
manik*) with beadwork applications.
Glass beads are a symbol of wealth
and power. The patterns represent* aso,
*highly stylised, mythical, dragon-like
creatures.*
51 × 48 cm

Indonesia, West Kalimantan,
Dayak Maloh people
*Ceremonial jacket (*sape manik*)
in cotton, with bark cloth lining;
glassbeads and brass pendants.
The anthropomorphic patterns
(*kakaletau*) represent spirits
and ancestors.*
51 × 46 cm

Indonesia, Kalimantan, Kenyah,
Kayan people
*Men's jacket in painted beaten bark-
cloth and needlework designs in cotton
fibres and dyed fringes.*
65 × 53 cm

Malaysia, Sarawak, Rejang River,
Iban Dayak people
*Warrior's jacket (*baju empuru*) covered
with fish-scales, sewn with vegetable
threads.*
52 × 29.5 cm

Indonesia, West Kalimantan,
Dayak Maloh people
*Ceremonial skirt (*kain buri*) in hand-woven cotton trade-cloth. Split shells sewn as human and* aso *motifs.*
50 × 48 cm

Opposite page
Malaysia, Sarawak,
Iban Dayak people
Ceremonial cotton sarong (kain kebat*) in warp* ikat, *decorated with sequins, beadwork and brass discs.*
45 × 45 cm

Opposite page
Malaysia, Sarawak, Iban people
*Ceremonial cotton hanging (*pua kumbu*), warp* ikat *technique with human motifs.*
240 × 76 cm

Indonesia, Sulawesi, To Kaili people
*Ceremonial dress (*halili petondu*)
in cotton with coloured star and mica
applications. Worn over a* sarong.
61 × 90 cm

Indonesia, Sulawesi, North Central
Area, To Kaili people
*Woman's dress (*halili petondu*) made
in cotton, with cotton applications;
beads and mica. Bark cloth lining.*
62 × 80 cm

Indonesia, Central Sulawesi
*Woman's dress (*lemba*) in bark-cloth
(*fuya*) with brown paintings. Worn
with a* sarong *for ceremonial occasions.*
56 × 84 cm

Indonesia, Sulawesi,
Kajang Bulu Kumba
*Large cotton shawl with coloured
supplementary weft decorations
of checks and flowers.*
280 × 150 cm

Opposite page
Indonesia, Sulawesi, Galumpang
*Toraja ceremonial cloth (*paporito
noling*) hand spun cotton yarn with
warp* ikat*, geometric ancestral motifs.*
166 × 151 cm

Pages 168-169
Indonesia, South Sumatra, Lampong
*Central detail of ceremonial cotton skirt
(*tapis*) with silk embroideries showing
anthropological and iconographical
motifs, mica decorations and* ikat *side
panels.*
120 × 146 cm

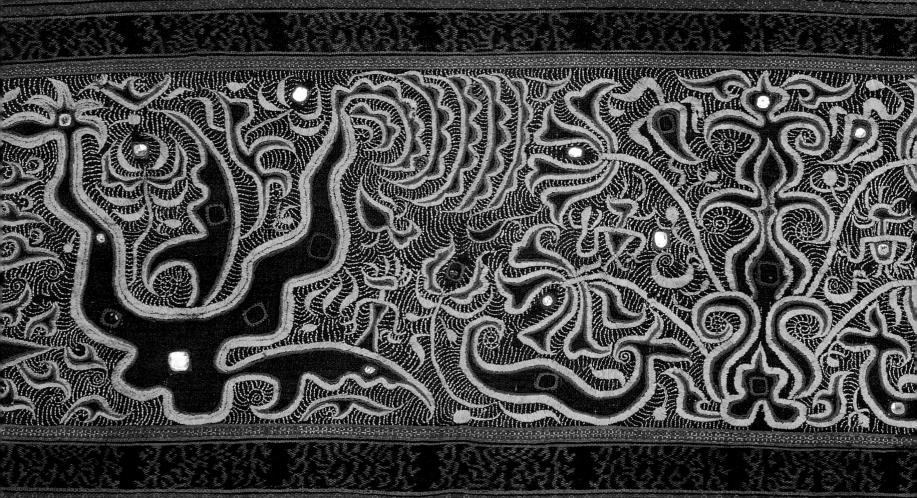

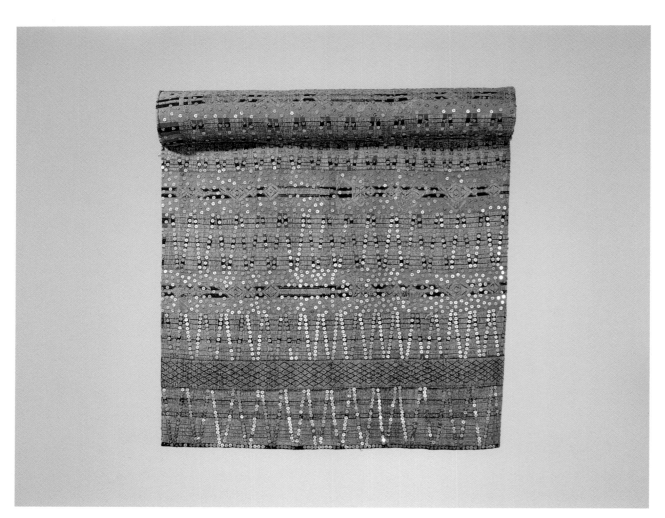

Indonesia, South Sumatra, Lampong
*Ceremonial skirt (*tapis*). Silk and
cotton striped ground, decorated with
geometric figures and bands. Metal
thread supplementary weft and sequins.*
125 × 100 cm

Indonesia, Sumatra, Lampong
*Ceremonial skirt (*tapis*) with two
cotton panels embroidered with silk
yarn and mica sequins. The embroidery
represents ships and humans. The other
sections are woven in silk and cotton.*
116 x 62 cm

Indonesia, South Sumatra, Lampong
*Ceremonial cotton skirt (*tapis*) with*
two silk embroidered bands showing
anthropological and iconographical
motifs, with four ikat *decorated panels.*
125 × 110 cm

Indonesia, Sumatra, Lampong,
Kauer people

*Cotton jacket worn by unmarried
women during their festival. The lapels
are embellished with tiny* cermuk
mirrors, silk threads and nussa *shell.*
30 × 150 cm

Ceremonial festive skirt (tapis) *in
cotton with silk embroideries, mica
decorations* (cermuk) *and weft* ikat.
137 × 114 cm

Opposite page: back detail of jacket

The back is in songket *supplementary
weft weave and metallic yarns.
The decoration uses the couching
technique.*

Left
Indonesia, Sumatra, Aceh
Trousers (bungkoih ranub) in silk and cotton with silver thread embroidery worn on festive occasions by men and women.
111 × 90 cm

Indonesia, Sumatra, Aceh
Trousers from Palembang in damasked silk with cotton waistband and lining. The embroideries are in silk and metallic threads with sequins and couched metal thread embroidery.
89 × 77 cm

Opposite page
Indonesia, Sumatra, Aceh
Silk and cotton shawl decorated all over with gold supplementary weft.
223 × 86 cm

Opposite page
Indonesia, Sumatra, Passemah
*Silk shawl (*slendang*) with
supplementary gold weft and brocaded
tapestry weave with* tirtanadi *edge.*
288 × 58 cm

Indonesia, Sumatra, Palembang
*Silk waistcoat with supplementary weft
and warp silk and metal threads;
applications of metal cord embroideries
with a plaited silk and metal gallon.*
52 × 150 cm

Opposite page
Indonesia, West Sumatra,
Minangkabau people
*Women's ceremonial silk head dress
(sampiran). Ground, red cotton warp
and black silk weft, with gold-wrapped
silk supplementary weft.*
280 × 48 cm

Indonesia, Sumatra, Tanjung
Sangaijan, Minangkabau people
*Check ground shawl or head dress. Silk
warp and cotton weft, borders are in
songket motifs with gold threads.*
88 × 57 cm

Indonesia, Sumatra, Palembang
Silk velvet court dancer's tunic (baju kurung) embroidered with silk and metal threads.
95 × 136 cm

Opposite page
Indonesia, South West Sumatra, Bengkulu

Young dancer's silk shawl, weft ikat, *supplementary silk and metal weft stripes, with edges in* songket.
252 × 113 cm

Brown silk shawl in tapestry weave, weft ikat *and supplementary weft metal thread with mica decorations.*
223 × 55 cm

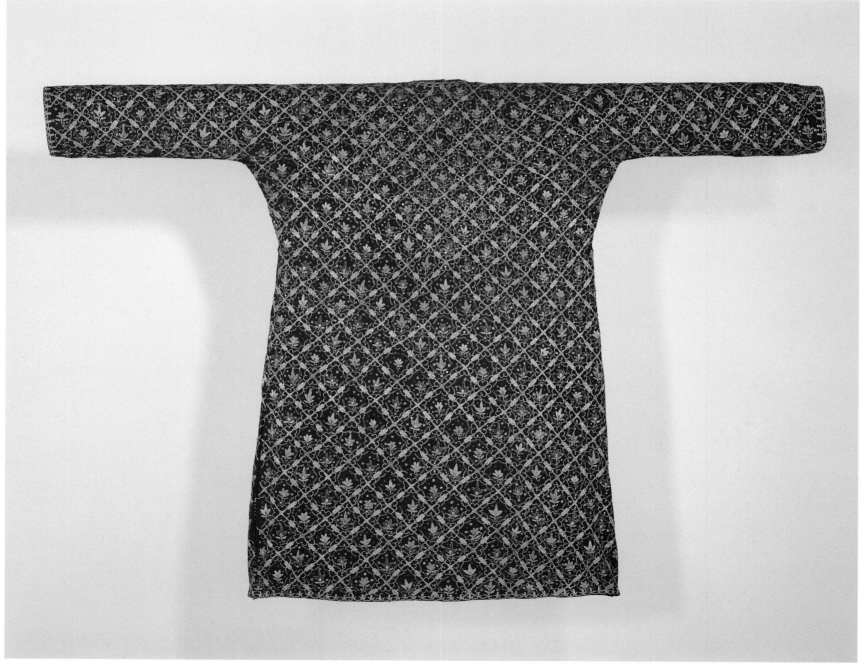

Indonesia, Centre Sumatra

Top
Karo Batak
Cotton shawl, warp ikat *and brocaded with human motifs.*
212 × 76 cm

Centre
Toba Batak people
*Silk warp and cotton weft sacred shawl (*ragidup*) woven in three sections with supplementary weft decoration.*
193 × 108 cm

Bottom
Toba Batak people
*Ceremonial shawl (*ragi hotang*) with three-colour warp* ikat *and supplementary weft twining*
210 × 96 cm

Opposite page
Indonesia, North Sumatra, Aceh

*Woman's blouse (*batu mesirat*) Sirat design. Different cotton cloths attached with machine embroidery.*
47 × 45 cm

*Cotton shawl (*slendang*) with supplementary gold weft thread: fringe is made of lead pendants and beads.*
170 × 56 cm

Indonesia, Sumatra,
Muntok Bangka Island
*Silk shawl (*limar*), with centre of very
fine red and yellow weft ikat,
surrounded by metal threads in* songket
decoration.
226 × 89 cm

Opposite page
From left to right
Indonesia, Sumatra, Palembang
*Red and green silk shawl (*kain plangi*),
made by* tritik *technique,* ikat *fringes
with needlework metal thread edges.*
172 × 79 cm

Opposite page
Indonesia, Sumatra, Palembang

*Silk shawl (*kain plangi*), made by* tritik
technique, worn on festive occasions.
200 × 84 cm

*Silk shawl (*kain plangi*), made by* tritik
technique, worn on festive occasions.
228 × 84 cm

Opposite page
Indonesia, East Sumatra, Palembang
*Silk ceremonial shawl (*limar*),
embroidery on the sides made of silk
and metal threads. The central motifs
are of fine weft* ikat.
200 × 85 cm

Indonesia, Java, Celanda

*Cotton child's trousers with coloured
batik print worn by a European or
Penenakan child.*
66.5 × 39 cm

Cotton batik sarong *with floral
decorations of European influence.*
106 × 99 cm

Opposite page
Indonesia, Java, Ceriban region,
(*kain panjang*)
Cotton hand-drawn batik Wadasan
*design for Japanese. Cloud or rock
design, (*mega mundung*).
248 × 102 cm

Indonesia, Java
*Cotton breastcloth (*kemben*), borders
in* batik. *Central part in* tritik
technique.
265 × 53 cm

Indonesia, Central Java, Surakarta
Breastcloth (kemben) *in silk and cotton*
batik (parang rusang) *motif reserved*
for royal families; silk application in
centre.
250 × 51 cm

Opposite page
Indonesia, Java
Detail of cotton batik *with popular life*
scenes and floral print decorations made
for Chinese market.
204 × 103 cm

Indonesia, Java, Yogjokarta, twentieth century
Bride's costume or court costume. The silk velvet tunic "baju" with silk lining is of European influence with applications of gold floral embroideries, sequins and gold ribbon. Worn on a batik sarong "kain panjong".
78 × 42 cm

Indonesia, Java, Yogjokarta
*Twentieth century man's court jacket
"baju" in wool, shows European
influence. Applications of gold floral
embroideries, ribbons and sequins.*
64 × 45 cm
Worn with a batik sarong "kain
panjong".
95 × 195 cm

Indonesia, Java

Blouse (kebaya) in fine cotton muslin with embroidery and lace decorations.
73 × 50 cm

Silk belt (gresik) pink silk weft ikat *and metallic weft threads. Court belt (dringin) from Surakarta.*
422 × 11.5 cm

Sarong *from Bali brocaded with gold threads, showing pea-cock motifs.*
274 × 150 cm

Opposite page
Indonesia, Bali, Singaraja

Men's waist-cloth worn on festive occasions, since the Balinese wear several clothes wrapped around the body. Silk and metallic yarn brocade (songket) *with supplementary weft.*
196 × 93 cm

Waist-cloth for men. Silk base, silk, silver, gold thread brocade (kain songket*) in supplementary weft. The* songket *production process is elaborate and time-consuming. These textiles are used for ceremony and dances.*
194 × 81 cm

Indonesia, Bali
Triangular silk breast cloth (kain
prada) *worn by dancers at special
festivals with sewn-on square patterns
decorated with gold leaf in floral motifs.*
152 × 90 cm

Indonesia, Bali
Silk sarong (kain prada*), worn by
women at weddings or when suffering
toothache and from part of a dancer
costume. The floral decoration is in gold
leaf.*
147 × 114 cm

Indonesia, Bali, Singaraja
*Women's shoulder-cloth (*slendang*) in silk and silver yarn, supplementary weft brocade and weft* ikat.
220 × 37 cm

Indonesia, Bali
*Women's shoulder-cloth (*slendang*) in silk and silver yarn, weft* ikat, *supplementary weft.*
248 × 38 cm

Indonesia, Bali
*Women's shoulder-cloth (*slendang*). Silk and metallic yarn, weft* ikat *and supplementary weft. These cloths are often associated with an Indian influence and court traditions.*
244 × 36 cm

Opposite page
Indonesia, Bali,
Tenganan pegeringsingan
Cotton double ikat *and embroidery (*geringsing*), in which resist patterns are applied to the warp and weft before weaving. Cotton and metallic yarn embroidery at each end.*
177 × 24 cm

Opposite page
Indonesia, Bali, Singaraja
Cotton belt with thirty-five alternations of warp ikat, *the weft taking the colour of the* ikat *each time. Supplementary weft in cotton and metallic yarns.*
420 × 18 cm

Indonesia, Bali
*Detail of open-work shawl (*tirtanadi*)
with three-colour supplementary weft
decorations in human motifs. Bebali
ceremonial fabric used to present new-
born babies to priests.*
274 × 41 cm

Opposite page
Indonesia, Bali
*Cotton breast-cloth (*kamben cerek*)
in spaced weaving technique
and supplementary weft. Worn by ladies
at temple ceremonies or during offerings
at house altar.*
124 × 36 cm

*Women's breast-cloth (*krang krang*)
in cotton spaced weaving technique.*
240 × 78 cm

Indonesia, Lombok
*Striped woven cotton shawl (*umbak
bolong*) with long fringes decorated
with Chinese coins.*
236 × 35 cm

Indonesia, East Sumba
*Man's cotton garment (*hinggi*) with
warp* ikat *and weft twining.*
234 × 110 cm

Indonesia, East Sumba,
Sumbanese people
*Woman's skirt (*lau pahudu*) with
variety of decoration techniques,
supplementary warp weave, warp* ikat,
*staining cotton. Showing human,
animal and geometric motifs.*
212 × 126 cm

Indonesia, Sumbawa
Cotton sarong. *Brocaded*
supplementary weft with metallic yarns
showing dragon and diamond motifs.
175 × 124 cm

Indonesia, Savu
Five-colour sarong *in heavy cotton worn at funerals. Warp and weft* ikat *floral and abstract motifs relating to the region.*
145 × 53 cm

Indonesia, Savu
Heavy cotton shawl in three-colour warp ikat *with butterfly, flower and abstract motifs.*
174 × 97 cm

Opposite page
Indonesia, Moluccas
Cotton shawl with multicoloured warp ikat *pattern and supplementary weft decorations. Tassels made with wrapped warp ends.*
288 × 37 cm

Indonesia, Timor, Amanuban
*Man's cotton loincloth (*selimut*), warp* ikat *showing anthropomorphic crocodile figures.*
162 × 43 cm

Indonesia, Timor, Amanuban
Part of a selimut *(side borders missing).* Warp ikat *showing anthropomorphic crocodile figures interrupted with geometrical motifs.*
177 × 38.5 cm
Detail on opposite page

Indonesia, Timor, Amanuban
*Man's cotton loincloth (*selimut*) in three panels. Central part is warp* ikat. *The two sides are in coloured stripes and warp* ikat.
186 × 100 cm + fringes

Indonesia, Timor, Atoni people
Women's sarong *in cotton and wool.*
Tai *with* futema *(human and animals*
motifs), supplementary weft in
geometrical motifs.
116 × 125 cm

Indonesia, Timor
Three panels cotton women's sarong
*decorated all over with coloured human
figures in supplementary weft.*
110 × 56 cm

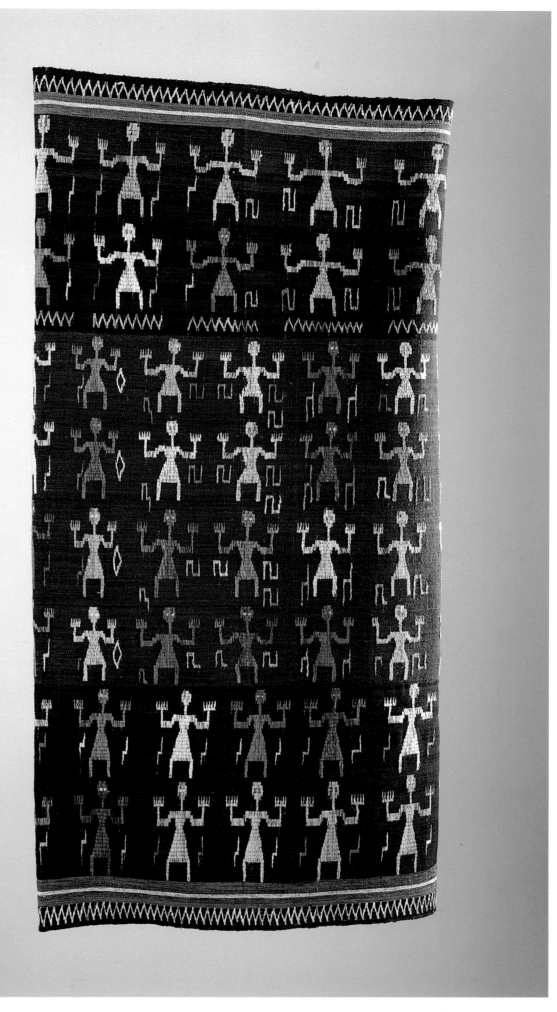

Indonesia, Timor
Royal cotton sarong *(selimut) woven in four panels, warp* ikat *with geometric supplementary weft motifs.*
162 × 54 cm

Indonesia, Timor
Cotton sarong *in four panels, decorated with very colourful supplementary weft geometric motifs and supplementary warp striped motifs.*
136 × 60 cm

From left to right
Indonesia, Timor
Man's cotton loincloth selimut, *woven in stripes with geometric supplementary weft motifs.*
168 × 91 cm
Detail on opposite page

Indonesia, Timor
Loincloth in three panels with supplementary warp stripe effects.
190 × 116 cm

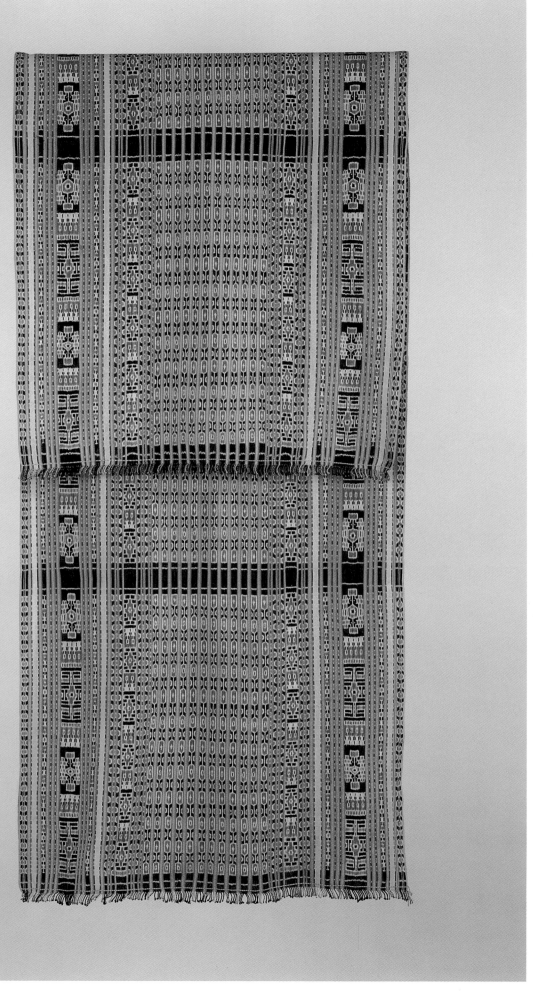

Indonesia, Timor
Men's cotton loincloth (selimut), with warp ikat *decoration.*
190 × 58 cm

Opposite page
Indonesia, Timor, Beti Mabuna
Men's cotton loincloth (selimut) in three panels. Elaborate central panel with anthropomorphic walking figures in supplementary weft, supplementary warp on side panels. Elaborate ones such as this were used by men of noble rank.
196 × 92 cm

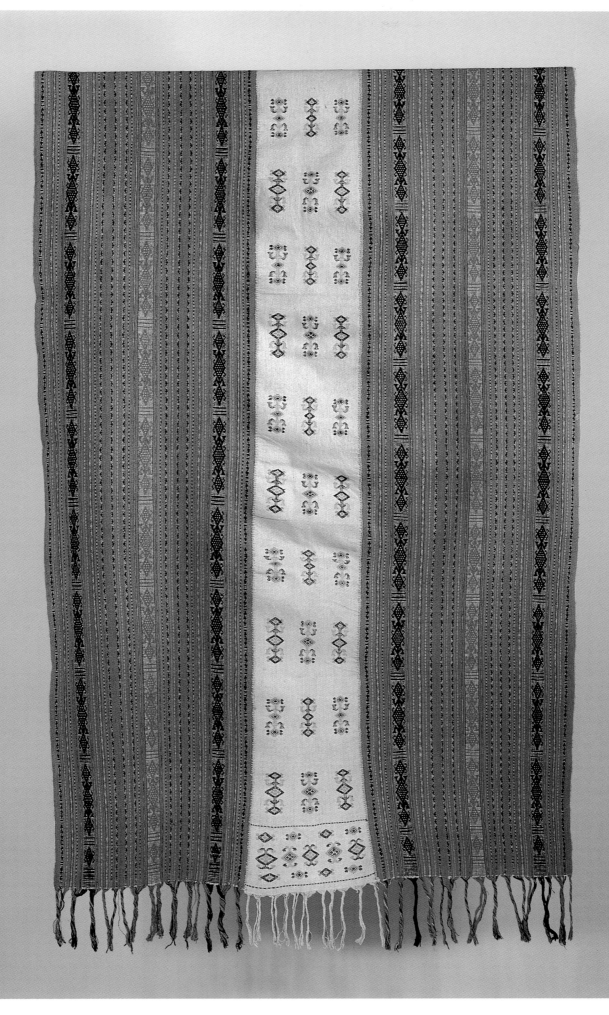

Opposite page
From top to bottom

Indonesia, Timor, Pilu Saluf

Cotton belt part of a hunter costume piece, long straps in tapestry weave, twining and plain weave.
206 × 185 cm

Ribbonned cotton belt part of a head-hunter costume piece with geometric supplementary weft decorations in tapestry weave, twining and plain weave.
196 × 115 cm

Cotton waistcloth, part of a head-hunter costume with supplementary weft decorations. Long straps in tapestry weave, twining and plain weave.
70 × 27 cm

Indonesia, Timor
Cotton straps decorated with glass beads and coins.
11 × 132 cm

Indonesia, Timor, Pilu Saluf
Men's loincloth in glass beads on cotton ground showing anthropomorphic and geometrical figures with long straps.
80 × 50 cm

Claudine Delecourt

Far East

Tibet
Ritual Buddhist monk dancer's apron decorated with appliqué *motifs of human heads, skulls, dorjey and a large central mask of the cruel god Khrorgyal, worn by the "Black Cap" lamas during the dance ceremonies of Yama, god of hell.*
97 × 74 cm

China. The Middle Kingdom.
The Silk Country

Since ancient times the textile industry has played an essential role in China's art and economy.

In legendary periods, the thwarted love of the two deities – the male Cowherd and the female Weaver, who are only allowed to meet one day a year – is a reminder of the division of the day's work between men and women. The man works in the field, and the woman stays at home and weaves. The Weaver is the Alpha star of the Lyra constellation, and weaves all year round by the side of the Milky Way. On the opposite side is the Bootes constellation, tilling his field and harnessed to the Chariot in Ursa Major.

Other legends describe how silk and weaving were invented. The legendary Sovereign Fuxi taught the people how to grow mulberry trees and raise silkworms. The Yellow Emperor's wife Si Lingchi (also named Leizi) discovered the secret of winding off the silk cocoon and taught it to her retinue.

China was the first nation to grow silk. Fragments of pieces of silk from the third millennium BC have come to light in Qingtai, Henan, Qianshanyang and Zhejiang. Under the Shan-Yin (1600-1100 BC) the Chinese were already experts at spinning silk. They used improved spinning mills and set up systems allowing silk to be woven in the Jacquard way. Fortune-telling inscriptions engraved on bones and tortoise shells found at Anyang show archaic forms of ideographs for the mulberry tree, silkworm and silk thread.

The Economics of Silk

The state was in control of the silk industry from the second millennium BC onwards. Silk fabrics were used to pay taxes and salaries and to purchase peace in the course of diplomatic negotiations. Emperors set up weaving and embroidery mills to satisfy the needs of their courts.

These institutions were managed by appointees of the Emperor whose mission was to provide the raw materials, pay the craftsmen and supervise the distribution of the finished products. The persons employed in these workshops included dyers, technicians, mechanics for the maintenance of the mills and pattern designers for embroidery and weaving.

Variety of Fabrics

Ancient China produced remarkable fabrics in silk, hemp, ramie, *pueraria* cotton and wool. Gauze, brocades, satins and velvets with bright colours, refined designs and a soft touch made up a line of fabrics of unsurpassed quality which were represented in a variety of weaves (taffeta, serge, satin, open-work or double-weave).

Silk tapestries

The "continuous warp and discontinuous weft" process discovered under the Eastern Zhou dynasty (722-481 BC) gave birth to the silk tapestry weaving method (or *kesi*), which achieved an unprecedented development with the Qing (1644-1911). The Imperial workshops used the *kesi* for dresses, folding screens, pillows, paintings, fans, lanterns, etc., for the Imperial family.

Embroidery

From the time of the Shang, Chinese women as well as men excelled in the art of embroidery. Some recorded names from the Ming times have come down to us. One of the most famous women is Han Ximeng from the Gu school. Ting Pei and Shen

Zhou, who lived in the nineteenth century, were famous male embroiderers.

Embroideries decorate garments and many objects, such as purses, shoes, glass-cases, banners and altar ornaments. As well as being a hobby for wealthy ladies, embroidery is a costly luxury. A glass-case fifteen centimetres long, for instance, needs more than twenty thousand embroidery points. The production of theatre costumes, mandarin robes or feminine garments takes ten to twelve workers four or five years. The Chinese have thirty-six different embroidery stitches and use both gold thread and knotted stitches in their work.

The Chinese Costume and Its Symbolism

From antiquity the garment and its ornaments reflect the wearer's position in society. The rite book of the Zhou stipulates that kings and officials must wear ceremonial garments for every rite. The five primary colours are reserved for the nobility. Ordinary people must use complementary colours.

The manner of dressing up reached its greatest complexity and variety under the Qing. That is why an illustrated catalogue (*Huangchao liqi tushi*) classifying all garments and accessories used by the Emperor, his court and even his lowliest official was brought out in 1759 under Emperor Qian Long. The last dynasty defended the values of Confucianism, Taoism and Buddhism. Like the Yuan (1260-1368), it also protected Tibetan Lamaism. It is for this reason that colour codes and ornamental designs of these various schools of thought are found to be combined on the textiles. Confucian philosophy states that young people should wear light-coloured garments and older people darker ones, thus defining everyone's place in society. Combinations of emblematic designs refer to the three doctrines: the "Eight Treasures of the Scholar", the "Eight Taoist Symbols of Immortality" and the "Eight Jewels of Buddhism".

Certain symbolic figures constitute a second language. For example, the peony – the queen of flowers – evokes wealth and nobility. Other motifs are based on word-plays in Chinese. Thus the similarity of sound between the character *fu* (happiness) and *bian fu* (bat) explains how the bat became the symbol of happiness. Similarly, the butterfly represents a twenty-year-old man. This butterfly symbolizes long life. Signs such as *shou* (longevity) and *xi* (joy) often appear on fabrics, as does the swastika, symbol of the infinite.

The Dragon Dress, the Official Court Garment

Dragon robes (*long pao*), worn by the nobility and the civil service, were particularly in fashion dur-ing the Qing period. They can be blue, turquoise, brown, orange, yellow or red. They were first mentioned in 694, when the Empress Wu rewarded her officials with this garment. Under the Song, the law allowed only the Emperor and the Empress to wear the dragon robe. The Mings continued the practice of Empress Wu and offered dragon robes as presents to heads of allied and vassal nations or as a reward for a worthy act. Corruption being then rampant, the government finally started selling the privilege of wearing the dragon robe. This became common practice at the end of the Qing. Under the reign of Emperor Dao Guang (1821-50) a price list was even published. Demand was such that the dresses had to be mass-produced. Merchants, missionaries and European civil servants wore them and high-class ladies used them as evening dresses.

The dragon robe is a cosmic diagram. The upper part shows the sky and the clouds in which the dragon, symbol of Imperial authority, is chasing the jewel, the symbol of perfection and knowledge. The inner edge of the garment, decorated by oblique bands and waves (*lishui*), represents the "Universal Ocean", from which Earth emerges in the form of three or five peaks.

The symbolism becomes complete when the garment is worn. The human body becomes the axis of the universe on which the forces of Earth and Sky align themselves. The collar suggests the Sky Gate, which separates the material world from the spiritual world, symbolized by the head of the wearer.

Women's Garments

In the seventeenth century, Emperor Qian Long suggested that the Liao, Jin, and Yuan dynasties had lost their power because their leaders had given up traditional Mongol dress in favour of Han fashions. The Manchus, who had been associated with the Han for a long time, had indeed let themselves be influenced by them, and in practice the differences in the way the two nations dressed were slight and tended to disappear at the end of the Qing dynasty. Manchu women wore long dresses (*pao*) extending down to the ankles. By contrast, the top wear of the Han Chinese (*ao*) could reach the knees or mid-calf and it was worn over trousers (*ku*) or leggings. One of the characteristics of the Qing costume is the abundance of decorative borders. These were first designed to prolong the life of the garment and were placed on the collar, the wrists and the borders, the points of greatest wear. Later, richly embroidered borders became a decorative element, the fashion for which culminated at the end of the nineteenth century in their covering almost the entire garment.

When going out, women draped themselves in a coat stopping at the knees; this was open in the middle and buttoned all the way down with wide sleeves. To complete their attire, they wore overalls of varying length. This beautiful garment of Manchu origin became particularly fashionable at the end of the Qing.

Ceremonial Dresses

Special garments had to be worn during certain ceremonies, such as weddings and funerals.

For weddings, red was the recommended colour. This was also the custom of the Peranakan Chinese of Malaysia. Their women, called "Nonya", had created a particular embroidery art for important occasions such as weddings, births and birthdays. They were inspired by the Chinese model but gave preference to certain designs, mainly flowers and birds. Human figures were nearly absent except for Taoist immortals, who were the exception. In addition to Chinese techniques, they also used gold thread (*tekat*) embroidery of Malay origin, which was suitable for velvet. The collar and the shoes were also part of the wedding attire, the latter being invariably flat and closed.

At the end of the nineteenth century, the "Nonya" introduced pearls from Venice or from China into their embroidery.

Shoes

Manchu women did not have bandaged feet but wore embroidered satin shoes with compensated soles in the shape of flower-pots. These were lined with grey cotton and had a band on top to ease the passage of the foot. The high wooden heels lengthened the figure but also served to avoid dirtying the bottom of the garment.

Tibet. Chinese Silk in the Land of Snow

Sparsely inhabited Tibet, a vast plateau in Central Asia, has seen the birth of an original civilization, principally influenced by Buddhism. Tibetan Lamaism extended its influence to Mongolia and China. Under the Qing dynasty many members of the Imperial family were leaders of the yellow bonnet sect. The close ties between Tibet and China since the Tang dynasty favoured the trade in silk and its importation. The Qing Emperors made sizeable gifts of silks and embroideries from Imperial workshops to monasteries. Tibetans took no notice of the symbolic subtleties of the designs of these silks and cut the garments from the fabric for their lay or religious elite.

Dancing Lama Apron (phan-kheb)

This apron, decorated with cut human heads, skulls, and dorjeys, has at its centre a fierce divinity (*Khro-rgyal*). It was worn by a dancer with a black hat during *charn*, an end of year temple rite performed by Lamas for three days to expel harm. At the end of the ceremony, the main performer, personifying Yama, the god of death, stabbed a human figure in paste placed in the courtyard of the monastery with his ritual dagger.

The dancer, armed with this ritual dagger (*phur-bu*) and wearing a skull-cap, wears an ample and sumptuous garment comprising a black hat, a heavy Chinese brocade dress, a collar, whose multi-lobed shape is reminiscent of clouds, and an apron.

Religious Garments

The monastic garment of the Tibetan monks is derived from that worn by Indian holy men, depending on local conditions and climate. The quality of the material varies according to its intended use, whether by the Dalai Lama or humble novices. The monk's robe, cut from a red woollen fabric, is worn together with a vest, a belt, a shawl, boots and a hat. The vest (*stod-gag*), which is often made up of pieces of brocade and has wide armholes bordered with dark red (*pulu*), is not part of the Indian monastic attire. It is worn by Tibetan monks of all schools and is thought to originate in Bengal.

Attire of the Lay High Official

The ancient Tibetan administration (*kashag*) is a nine-tiered hierarchy, the lay and religious officials being members of the hereditary nobility.

The lay officials wore satin or brocade garments. The fabrics and colours would vary in accordance with circumstances, hierarchical position and the season. The official's attire was made up of a double-breasted robe (*chuba*), shirt, belt, boots and hat. The robe can be cut in a piece of yellow background silk tapestry (*kesi*) with dragon and cloud designs. Some pieces of *kesi* used for these robes were originally meant for the Imperial family but had been rejected as faulty and used as gifts from the Qing emperors to the Tibetan princes.

Although the dragon robe was no longer worn in China after the fall of the Qing (1911), it is still in use in Mongolia and Tibet. Monasteries still own dragon robes, which are worn during festivals. Tibetan officials hang a bottle-holder, a knife and an embroidered purse to their belt, which is a essential accessory.

Both Tibetan and Chinese officials would change hats and garments at fixed dates without reference to the weather. Summer attire is worn from the eighth day of the third month, and winter attire from the twenty-fifth day of the tenth month, which is the anniversary of the death of Tsong Kah-Pa. The round winter hat of the Tibetans and Manchus is derived from the fur-lined cap with turned-over sides worn by the nomads.

Japan. The Land of the Rising Sun

Japan is a land of contrasts of hot and cold. The beauty of its nature cannot efface the disasters which afflict it, such as volcanic eruptions, typhoons and earthquakes. In the same way, the Japanese people are a blend of elements, having their prehistoric origins in different parts of the Asian continent: Siberia, Mongolia and the islands of Indonesia. Nowadays, modern life rubs shoulders with popular traditions stemming from mythological times. Both jeans and *kimonos* are to be seen in the street. Strictly speaking, the word *kimono* means dress, but today it is used strictly to denote the Japanese national costume as worn by both men and women. Too restrictive and impractical for an active way of life, it is essential for use as a ceremonial dress, being worn at weddings, festivities and funerals. It has a history going back a thousand years.

Monk's Robes

From China, Buddhism in the sixth century entered Japan, where it became a source of inspiration for artists and made its mark on everyday life. The manner of dress of the different Japanese sects was largely similar. Monks wore a white narrow-sleeved *kimono* under a wide-sleeved robe (*dofuku*). This is completed by a rectangular piece of fabric (*kesa*), the symbol of Buddhism. It has its origins in the robe of the Indian monks (Sanskrit: *kasaya*). The *kesa* is made up of a number of pieces of cloth with close overstitches (*sashiko*). It must be sewn as an act of mediation, by the monk or layperson who will wear it, and may consist of anything from five to twenty-five pieces. The *kesa* is a sort of *mandala*. Its four corners denote the four points of the compass, while the tree squares in the centre represent Buddha and two of his disciples. The monks frequently own three *kesa*. For important ceremonies, they wrap a richly woven *kesa* around their waist. The straps knotted round the shoulders are broad, flat pieces similar to those that decorate the *kesa* itself. The monks usually use gold brocade (*kinran*) for these, the warp being made of silk and the weft of gold.

Pilgrim's Robes

Pilgrims wear white robes to travel from temple to temple, and it is in these robes that their prayers are borne. Of the many pilgrimages that exist in Japan, one of the most famous is that of Kukai, the founder of the esoteric Shingon sect.

Kukai, also known as Kobodaishi, was born on the island of Shikoku in 774 and is one of the most striking figures of Japanese history. A calligrapher, engineer and inventor of the *kana* script, he went to China in order to extend his studies of Buddhism and the Sanskrit script of Siddham. Some pilgrims who follow in the footsteps of Kukai take six weeks to go to all of the eighty-eight temples on the island on foot. They wear robes of white cotton or raw hemp decorated with stamps, seals and woodprints indicating the names of the temples they have visited.

Many robes bear the image of Kobodaishi and Fudo Myo-o. Kobodaishi is shown sitting on a Chinese chair holding a *vajra* in his right hand and a rosary in his left. Fudo Myo-o can be seen in the vertically held dagger, around which is entwined a dragon engulfed in flames. His worship and images were introduced into Japan by Kukai. Fudo Myo-o personifies steadfastness of spirit and determination to annihilate evil. Ordinary people call on him to help them ward off impurity, sickness and malevolence.

Short Tunics

The Japanese have a number of short tunics that they wear over the *kimono* or with the *hakama* and leggings. Worn by all sections of society, the *kaori*, which made its appearance during the Momoyama period (1573-1603), is one of the most interesting Japanese items of attire because it is always worn in conjunction with whatever is contemporary. The *haori*, the official dress for private invitations, became in the seventeenth century a tunic for outdoors worn over the *kimono* by people from all walks of life, its length varying depending on the current fashion. Cut similarly to the *kimono*, it is closed at the front by means of cords hid in a number of different ways (*munahimo*). Much favoured by *geishas* and women in general, the *haori* is to them an everyday garment that is not suitable for ceremonies.

The *hanten*, a short tunic, was worn by male workers during the Edo period as a protection against the cold. The collar is not folded over and does not have any cords.

The Edo merchants made their workers wear the *happi*, a kind of *hanten* with the name of the merchant's shop painted on the collar, the back and the breast. This costume is nowadays worn at festivities.

To protect themselves when carrying out their du-

China
Peasant's palm fibre rain costume, worn by rice pickers, with cape and apron skirt.
220 × 120 cm

ties, firemen wore a balaclava helmet and a heavy quilted cotton *hanten* bearing the insignia of their brigade. They were recruited from among carpenters because of their skill in handling ladders and using axes to enter ruined buildings. There were forty-eight fire-brigades in Edo. In a city where the houses are made of wood, fire is an ever-present threat. Fires such as those known as "Edo flowers" caused enormous damage: that in 1657 cost the lives of 107,000 inhabitants and destroyed 15,000 houses.

Making a Kimono

The cut of the *kimono* has remained the same for centuries. Seven straight pieces are cut from a strip of material twelve metres long and between thirty-three and thirty-eight and a half centimetres wide; these are then sewn together side by side. Folds are sewn into the shoulders of *kimonos* to be worn by children, and the difference in length are likewise allowed for by similar folds at the waist.

Wearing the Kimono

The *kimono* varies depending on the age of the wearer. Young unmarried girls wear *furisode* with very long sleeves. On the day of their wedding, they use two *furisode*, one white and the other of some other colour. As they advance in age, the Japanese wear increasingly dark-coloured *kimonos* made of fine cloth. The *montsuki*, which are *kimonos* bearing the family coat-of-arms (*mon*), are reserved for ceremonial occasions. The *mon* are block-printed in white on each shoulder, one on each sleeve and one in the middle of the back. Some motifs are preferred by women, such as the "Three Companions of Deepest Winter" – pine, bamboo and plum trees (*sho*, *chiku*, *bai*) – symbolizing longevity. The colours also have a meaning, indigo being reputed to cure diseases of the skin, while red is supposed to be good for the eyes.

Accessories

To the Japanese clothes are an adornment, and for this reason, right from the Heian period (754-1185) they no longer wore jewellery. However, since the *kimono* has no pockets, they hang one or two richly worked accessories from its belt or slip them into the sleeves and neck opening. The most popular of these accessories are *inro*, or little medicine boxes, but they also use a wide range of other objects such as purses, bags holding good luck charms, sewing kits and tobacco pouches. The use of tobacco, which was introduced into Japan by the Portuguese at the end of the sixteenth century, rapidly became widespread, and by the sev-

enteenth century men and women of all sections of society were smoking pipes. These acquired the status of essential conversation accessories and for smoking outside people hung on their belts a leather or fabric tobacco pouch (*tabako ire*), linked by little chains to a *manju netsuke*, in the form of a large convex button, and a box (*zutsu*) containing the pipe (*kiseru*).

During the Edo period, gifts were sent in *fuku-sa*, which were squares of finely decorated thick satin with a silk lining. At first the *fuku-sa* always had to be returned to the person who had sent the gift but ultimately they were employed as handbags, the only limit to the uses to which they were put being the imagination of the owner. The possessions and presents of a bride were taken to her new home wrapped in *furoshiki*, large, finely decorated rectangular pieces of fabric.

Obi

The *kimono* has no buttons and is closed by a belt (*obi*) slung between the breast and the hips. The *obi* is the focal point of a person's attire and attracts the attention of others. Its beauty is highlighted by its colours, weave and decorations, which lend it an air of harmony. Women's *obi* are four or five metres long and about thirty-five centimetres wide. Men wrap round their waist an *obi* ten centimetres wide at the most. The *obi* become narrower as the wearer increases in age. There are up to five hundred ways of tying it. *Obi* are different depending on the season or if they are worn with a ceremonial dress. Summer *obi*, made of gauze lined with silk, are lighter. The most valuable ones are worn with the nuptial *kimono* (*manu obi*). The *fukuro obi* is not reversible; it is lined with a simple-coloured material and decorated with motifs in two or three places.

The three main forms are based on the drum (*otaiko*), the plover (*chidori*) and the butterfly (*cho*). The *kimono* is closed by placing the left side over the right. The reverse order, as used by Westerners, is only employed for the version worn by the deceased at funerals.

Popular Art in the Tokugawa Period 1603-1868

In the 1920s, Yanagi Sôetsu (1889-1960) discovered the popular art of the Tokugawa period, which the aesthetes of the Meiji era had neglected. During the two and a half centuries during which Japan was shut off from the outside world, artisans had the opportunity to perfect their techniques. They worked for the aristocracy and well-to-do merchants but also for ordinary people. The fabrics, colours and decorations they created enriched everyday life and were a source of inspiration for modern designers.

During the pre-industrial period, silk was reserved for the upper classes, so that the Japanese were obliged to make materials on the basis of fibres obtained from bark or wood from trees such as the wisteria, the mulberry, the banana tree, the ramie or *pueraria hirsuta* (*kuzu*).

Cotton-growing was introduced with success in the sixteenth century. Peasants cultivated it as a means of payment and also in order to make their clothes and beds (*futon*). After spinning and weaving the cotton in their houses, they gave it to professional dyers for final processing.

Tsutsugaki, the most widespread technique employed, is similar to *batik* and is well suited to motifs applied by hand. Use is also made of block-printing (*katazome*), the production of which required the skills of a specialist.

Finally, the *ikat* process (*kazuri*) was particularly popular in metropolitan Japan in the seventeenth century and afterwards. Originating in India, *ikat* spread to South-East Asia and from there to Japan via the Ryukyu Islands. After 1611, when the islands became a Japanese vassal state, the *shoguns* demanded an annual tribute of *ikat*, cotton and vegetable fibre.

China
Uncut man's semiformal court robe
(jifu) in gold-brocaded silk with nine
dragons (kesi).
148 × 76 cm

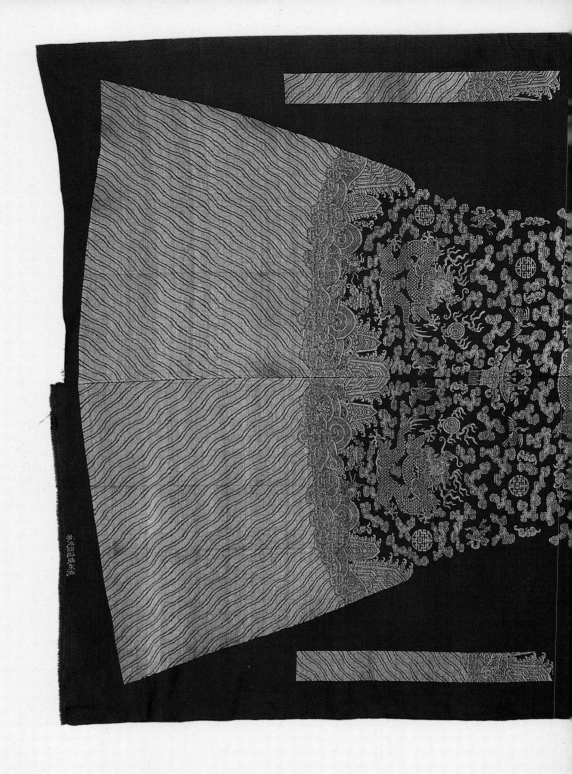

China, Han
Woman's semiformal domestic short summer coat (ao), in embroidered gauze and decorated with different galloons and applications; worn over trousers or leggings (ku).
98 × 150 cm

Opposite page
China, Manchu style
Woman's informal silk dress (pao) with tapestry woven coloured butterflies, borders with woven and embroidered galloons.
138 × 142 cm

China
Embroidered satin silk headband with four cabochons covered with ornament of kingfisher's feathers.
46 × 11 cm

Opposite page
China, Manchu style
Woman's informal sleeveless summer coat in silk gauze (kesi), woven with tapestry medallion motifs. Woven and silk-embroidered galloons on borders.
138 × 62 cm

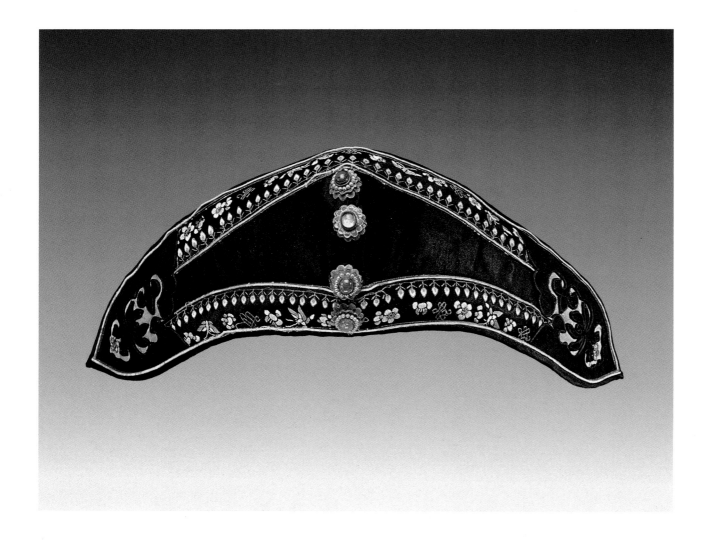

China, Manchu style
*Woman's informal dress (*pao*) with
flower and bird embroideries and
woven and embroidered galloons;* ruyi
design embroideries on waist.
142 x 154 cm
Detail on opposite page

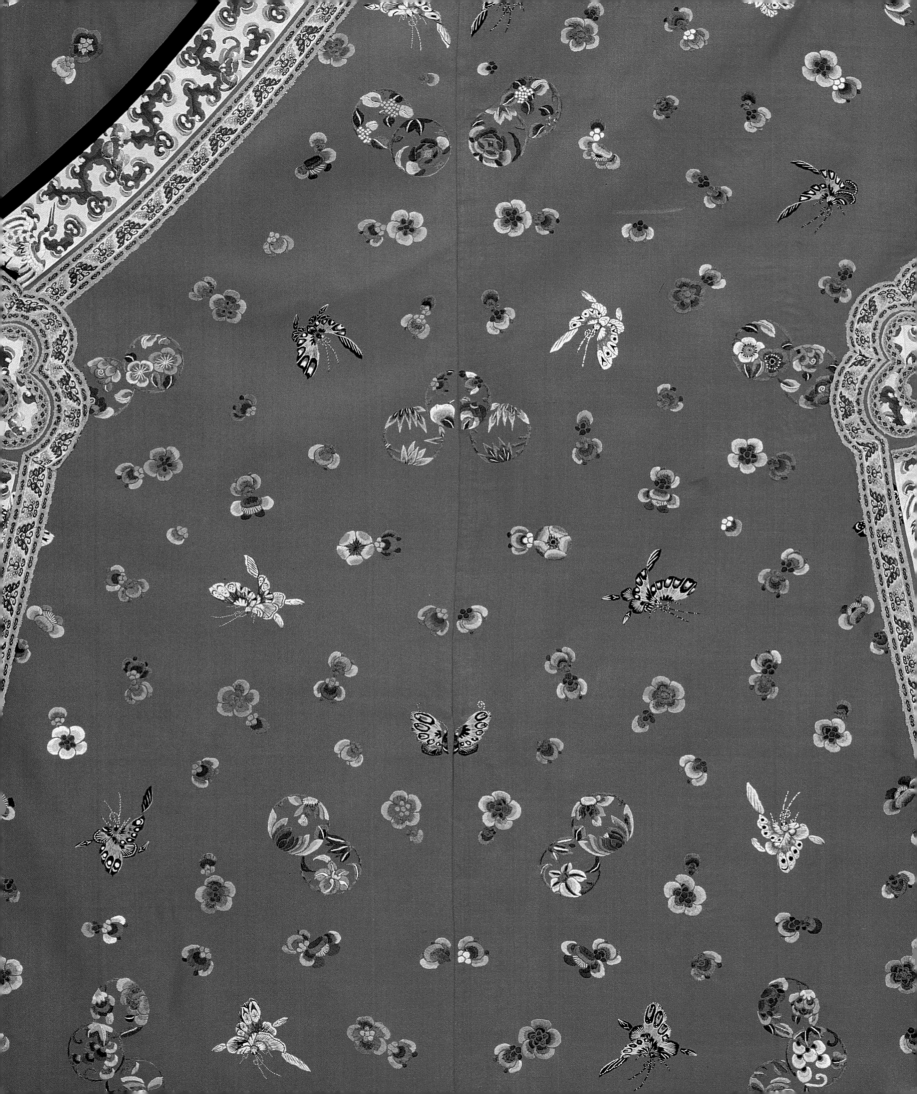

China, Han
*Woman's semiformal silk surcoat
(*waitao*) with floral embroideries;
the lower part shows the embroidered
symbol of the Ocean and the emerging
Earth.*
142 × 188 cm
Detail on opposite page

China, Peranakan, Manchu style

Bridal costume worn by Malaysian Chinese community. The brocaded silk dress has a silk lining and couched embroideries with floral motifs with silk and metal threads.
107 × 170 cm

The silk pleated skirt is similarly overembroidered.
98 × 50 cm

The multi-petalled large phoenix collar reminiscent of feathers, has embroidered its female figures; each petal is finished with a fine silk edge.
28 cm wide, 110 cm long

The shoes are in leather and silk velvet, embroidered with metal threads and sequins.
24 × 8 cm

China
*Woman's semiformal, brocaded velvet silk surcoat (*waitao*) with floral motifs; cuffs with floral embroideries, silk lining.*
150 × 175 cm

China, Guangxu
Block-heel woman's shoes (xie) of flowerpot design to keep coat hems clean. Heel covered with cotton, tip of shoe in satin silk with plaited and embroidered ribbons and cords.
25 × 8 cm, 16 cm high

Opposite page
China
A group of silk pouches in a variety of embroideries: flowers, plants, birds, houses; in knot stitch, winding stitch, pulling stitch and couching. Fine edgings, with pendants, plaited silk piping and tassels.
15 × 9 cm without pendants;
35 × 9 cm with pendants

China, Mongolian
*Woman's needlework cotton face veil
with a gold border and decorated with
plaited gold passementerie coral bead
strings and silk tassels.*
34.5 × 28 cm

China, Guizhan Miao people

Cotton baby-carrying pad with silk embroideries in medallion motifs.
65 × 65 cm

Cotton baby-carrying pad, wax print with medallion motifs.
76 × 66 cm

Opposite page
China, Guizhan Miao people
Detail of cotton baby-carrying pad,
wax print with spiral and cloud motifs.
60 × 32 cm

China, Guizhan Miao people
Cotton vest with silk embroideries and
wax printed with solar wheel motifs.
69 × 64 cm

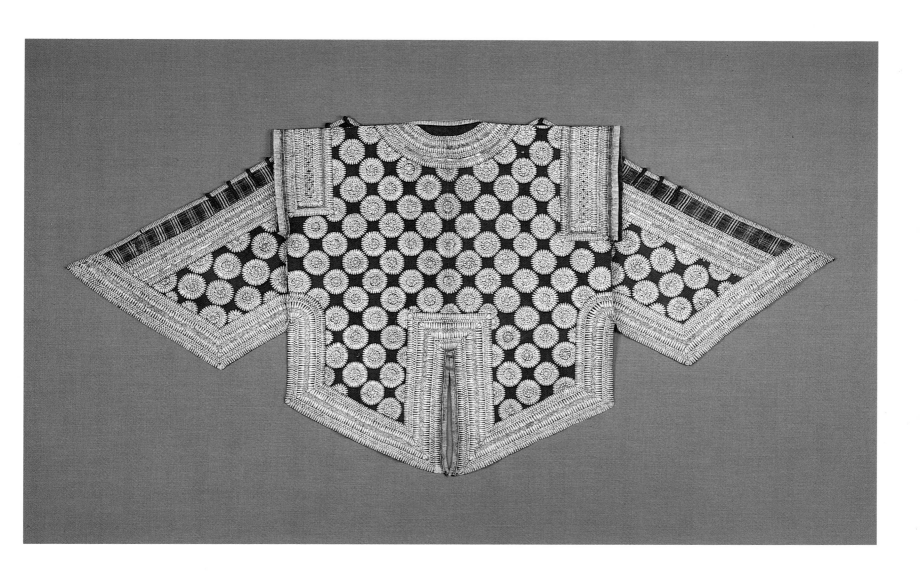

China, Guizhan Miao people from Huangping
Festive costume: jacket in figured satin silk mainly decorated on back and sleeves with horizontal and vertical multilayers of woven, embroidered silk strips. Lining is indigo-dyed and beaten shiny brown cotton.
70 × 150 cm

— *Pleated skirt in indigo-dyed beaten, powdered shiny cotton with four layers of woven and embroidered patterns on hem.*
75 × 260 cm

— *Apron is in indigo-dyed and beaten powdered shiny cotton with floral embroideries.*
50 × 45 cm

— *Belt has multilayered strip decoration on the side, pleated on the center and stitched.*
250 × 9 cm

China, Guizhan Miao people from
Huangping

Back decoration of jacket on p. 246.

Tibet

Cotton skirt decorated with applications of eighteen vertical embroidered silk bands with flower, bird and fish motifs, metal threads and discs. Embroideries are in knot stitch, winding stitch and pulling stitch. The lower part has a border of plaited and handpainted leather and metal strips.

77 × 93 cm

Opposite page

Tibet

Buddhist monk's vest (stod-gag) worn over the red woollen robe and made of different pieces of brocade with wide arm holes; yoke bordered with dark red pulu.

65 × 50 cm

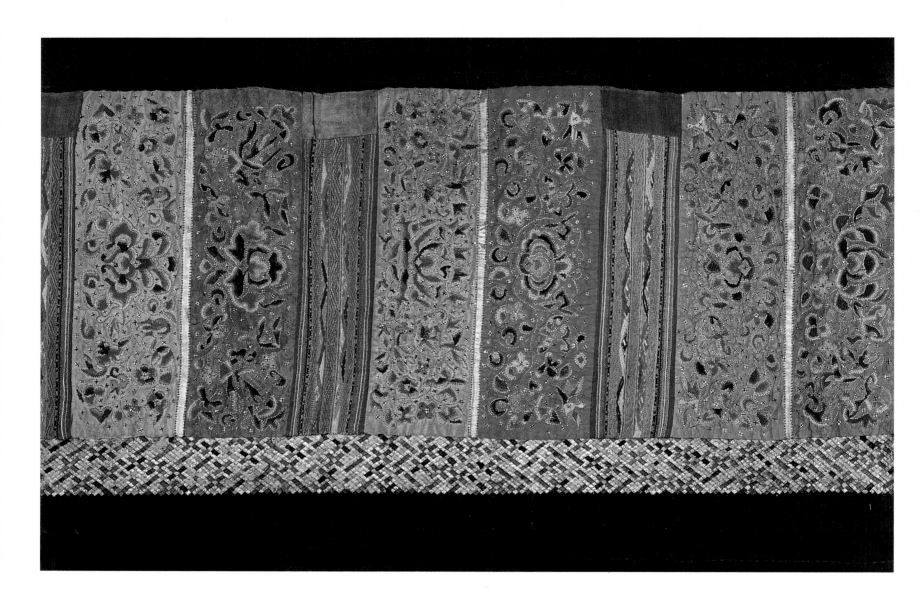

Tibet
*Satin silk tapestry coat (*kesi*) with cloud motifs and red silk lining.*
58 × 100 cm
Opposite page: detail of tapestry weave (*kesi*)

Japan
Buddhist priest's apron (kesa) in silk brocade made of several pieces of fabric symbolising the Buddhist vows of poverty. The repeating gold and silk medallion patterns have leaf and flower motifs with four square applications on each corner. The kesa is worn under the left arm and fastened on the right shoulder with the belt and cords.
146 × 56 cm

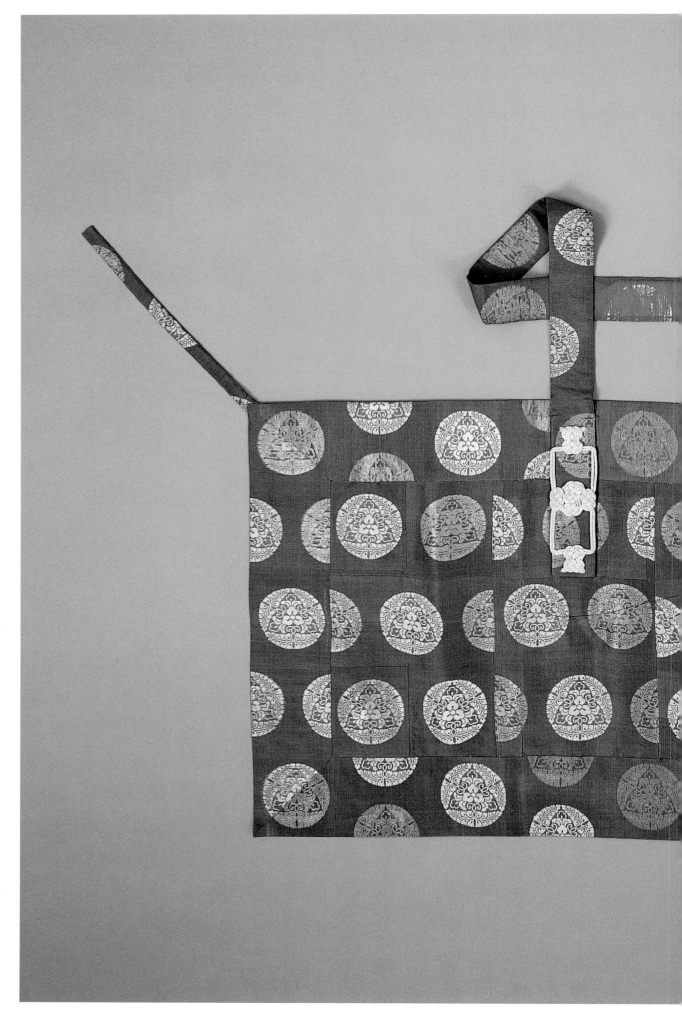

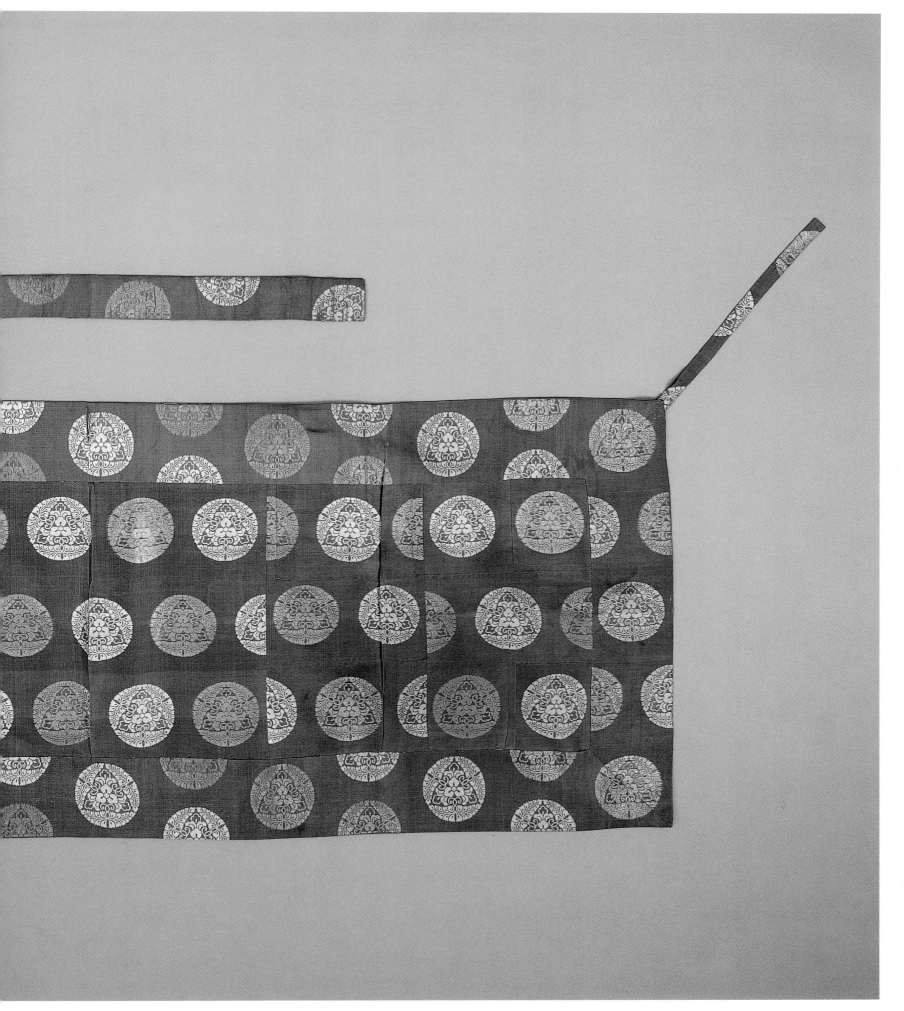

Japan
Kimono *in damasked silk, decorated with couched gold and silk thread embroideries, interior made of wadding and a red silk lining.*
156 × 90 cm
Opposite page: detail of couched embroideries

Opposite page
Japan
*Woman's sash (obi) in two layers of silk
cloth, woven with gold-wrapped silk
thread and brocaded with three floral
motifs.*
182 × 29 cm

Japan
*Okinawan banana fibre kimono, warp
and weft ikat (kasuri) with diagonal
and check effects.*
138 × 118 cm

Opposite page
Japan
Woman's fancy silk kimono *decorated with tie dye motifs (*shibori*) and silk lining.*
141 × 150 cm

Japan
*Brocaded woman silk sash (*obi*) decorated with coloured shrimp motifs.*
200 × 35 cm

Japan
Front of short banana fibre coat
(haori)*, worn by pilgrims visiting*
Shinto shrines, showing the name of the
shrine, hand-written in sumi ink.
111 × 142 cm

Japan
Yukata summer kimono *in plain
weave ramie for high-born child. Rice-
paste resist and hand-painted ink
drawings (*sumi*) showing vegetable
motifs and wild boars.*
115 x 120 cm
Opposite page: detail of ink drawings
(*sumi*)

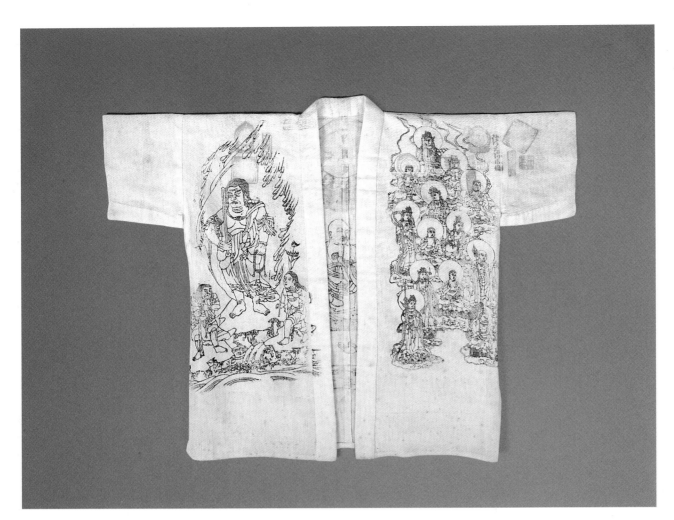

Japan
The Kûkai pilgrims who go to Shikoku island wear a special linen coat (ohenro-gi) *bearing the stamps of the Buddhist shrines visited by them (eighty-eight stamps for eighty-eight temples).* (Showing front and back).
67 × 85 cm

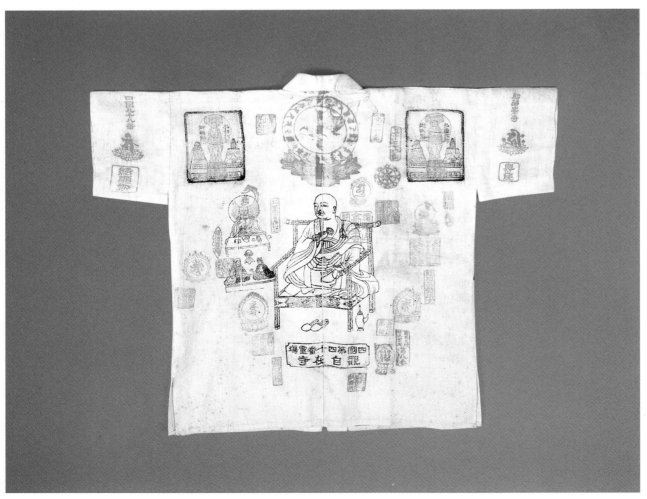

Opposite page
Japan
Front of a Kûkai pilgrim's coat.
98.5 × 106 cm

Page 266
Japan
Woman's summer kimono *in vegetable fibre with warp and weft* ikat *bearing abstract and cosmic motifs.*
140 × 120 cm

Page 267
Japan
Man's silk kimono, *covered all over by the* shibori *tie-dye technique, giving a crimped polka-dot surface texture ; silk lining with hand-painted decoration on the borders.*
155 × 142 cm

Japan
Indigo-dyed cotton kimono *made of three layers of fabric tightly quilted together with thick cotton threads; innermost layer shows stripes.*
96 × 148 cm

Japan
Omi *Okinawan. Double* ikat
*(*i-kasuri*) child's linen* kimono,
*with crossing striped designs of flowers
and birds.*
88 × 98 cm

Japan, Edo period
Front of fireman's coat (kaji Banten) in different layers of quilted cotton fabric (sashiko). Rice-paste resist, painted pigments, with designs on cotton lining.
95 × 140 cm

Japan, Edo period
Back of fireman's coat showing the graphic design identifying his brigade.
95 × 140 cm

Opposite page
Japan
Hat of fireman's costume made of different layers of quilted cotton fabric and striped lining.
55 × 32 cm

Japan (Hikoshi-Banten), Edo period,
nineteenth century
*Double-face fireman's coat in quilted
cotton layers. The back of the jacket
bears the identifying stencilled character
of the brigade. The hand-painted lining
shows a carp jumping over a waterfall,
an emblem of courage.*
93 × 129 cm
Opposite page: detail showing
the painted jumping carp

Japan, Meiji period

*Back of woollen fire coat (*kajibaori*). Applications of family coats-of-arms on each sleeve and on the back, made of a felt. The silk-lined coat has a long slit in the middle of the back. Silk and metal thread edging on borders.*
97 × 125 cm

Belt piece shows same felt made family sign and decorations.

These coats were used to protect the wearers as they escaped from burning buildings and were also worn at some ceremonial occasions too.

Opposite page
Japan, Meiji period
*Four chest protectors (*muna-ate*) worn under fire-coats (*kajibaori*). They are made in wool with felt applications and motifs showing the family coat-of-arms, with trimmings, silk edgings and neck bands.*
28 × 57 cm long

Japan, Meiji period
*Front of a camel-hair fire-coat
(*kajibaori*). The back shows the family
coat-of-arms in silk with silk trimmings
and fine silk edgings on the borders.*
95 cm × 120 cm

*The chest protector (*muna-ate*) is in
camel-hair decorated with silk
applications and the same family coat-
of-arms, with trimmings, silk edgings
and neck bands.*
28 × 57 cm

*These coats were used to protect the
wearers as they escaped from burning
buildings and were also worn at some
ceremonial occasions.*

Appendix

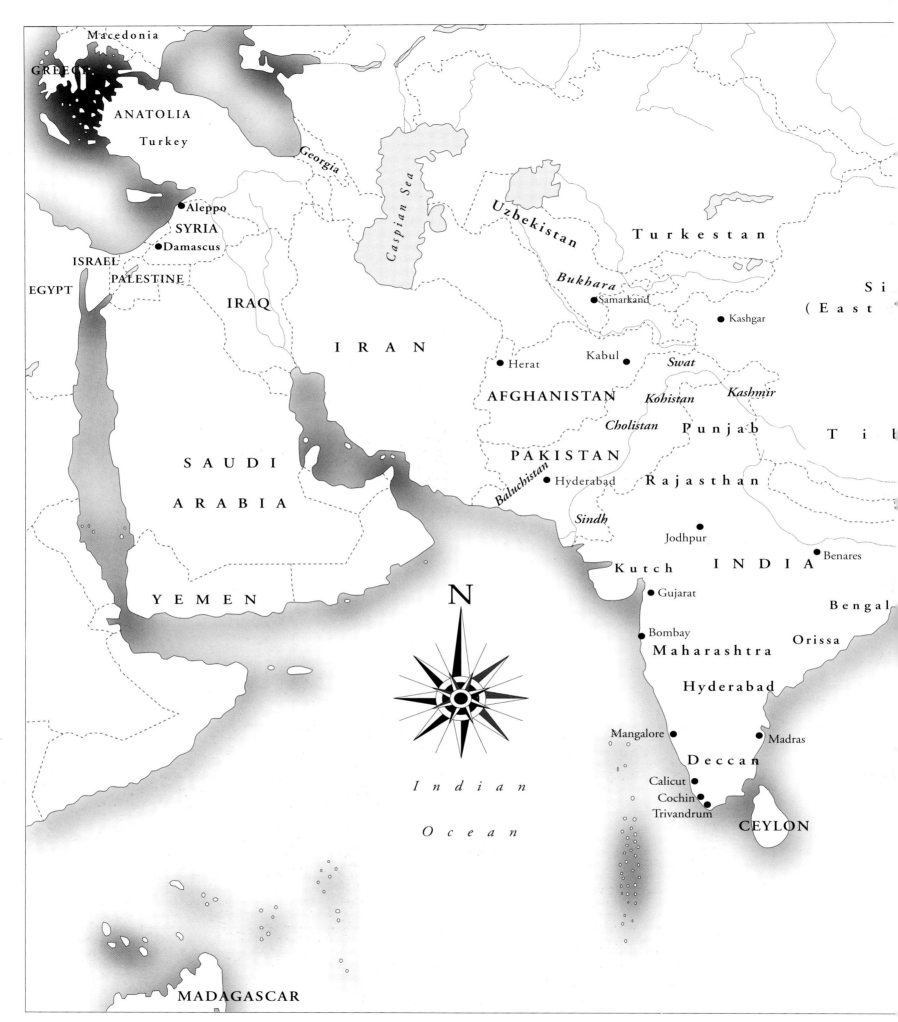

Macedonia

GREECE

ANATOLIA

Turkey

Georgia

Caspian Sea

Uzbekistan

T u r k e s t a n

●Aleppo

SYRIA

●Damascus

Bukhara

S i

(E a s t

●Samarkand

●Kashgar

ISRAEL

EGYPT

PALESTINE

IRAQ

I R A N

●Herat

Kabul●

Swat

AFGHANISTAN

Kohistan

Kashmir

Cholistan

P u n j a b

T i

SAUDI

PAKISTAN

●Hyderabad

R a j a s t h a n

ARABIA

Baluchistan

Sindh

Jodhpur

I N D I A

●Benares

Kutch

YEMEN

N

K u t c h

●Gujarat

B e n g a l

●Bombay

Maharashtra

Orissa

Hyderabad

Mangalore●

●Madras

D e c c a n

Indian

Calicut●

Cochin●

Ocean

Trivandrum

CEYLON

MADAGASCAR

280

Hokkaido

JAPAN

M o n g o l i a

Kyoto •

Kyushu

Amami Oshima

Ayukyu
Islands

ang

kestan)

Honan

Okinawa

t

Fukiea

Miyako
Yagiama Islands
Yohacuna

C H I N A

Kansu

Kweichow

TAIWAN

Yunnan

Luzon

PHILIPPINES

BURMA

Hainan

*P a c i f i c
O c e a n*

LAOS

alf

ngal

THAILAND

Mindanao

VIETNAM

*Visayan
Islands*

daman
lands

CAMBODIA

Lake Sebu

**West
Irian**

Minahasa

Kelantan

Sarawak

• Atjeh

MALAYSIA

Donggala •

SULAWESI

Medan •

Malacca

Celebes

S u m a t r a

B o r n e o

*Tanimbar
Islands*

Kisar Islands

Djambi •

•

*Lampung
Bay*

Flores

Babar Islands

Palembang

Bantam

Madura

Sumbawa

Timor

Bali

Surakarta

Lombok

Sumba

Roli

281

Glossary

Aba
Heavy cotton or woollen mantle worn by urban males in the Middle East, Palestine and Saudi Arabia. In Syria, a light men's tunic or coat. In some regions worn by women, who drape it over their heads. Tunic-shaped dress worn by Indian Moslem women over trousers.

Ad khin
Cotton breast-cloth with geometric motifs in supplementary silk weft, worn by the Kami people from Burma.

Ambi
Floral embroidery motifs used to decorate the front borders of coats from Kashmir.

Angrakha
Brocaded long silk man's robe with sleeves.

Ao
Short Chinese summer coat worn by women.

Aso
Dayak people's stylized pattern representing mythical dragon-like creatures.

Baju
South-East Asian outfit composed of a shirt or blouse with a *sarong*.

Baju empuru
Warrior's jacket covered with fish scales worn by Iban Dayak people.

Baju kurung
Silk velvet dancer's tunic from Palembang.

Baju-Java
Man's or woman's woollen court jacket from Jogjakarta showing European influence.

Bandhani
India. Gujarati term for resist tie-dyeing.

Banni
Special embroidery stitches showing floral designs on Kutch robes.

Batu mesirat
Woman's blouse worn by Aceh people.

Bebali
Ceremonial clothes for gods and men worn in Bali.

Bhoteh
Horn or bean-shaped shrub motif of Persian origin commonly used on Indian and Central Asian textiles.

Bisht
See aba.

Blaan sawal
Trousers made of vegetable fabric worn by Bogobo people from Philippines.

Bohça
High-quality wrapping material used for offerings or for storing clothes in the Middle East.

Bundi
Dot motifs applied by tie-dyeing on light cotton turbans of Rajasthan.

Bungkoih ranub
Embroidered festive trousers worn by Aceh people.

Buta
Embroidered floral motifs.

Cermuk
Small mirror pieces fixed on the cloth by embroidery.

Chadar
Swat women's shawl, decorated with floss silk embroideries.

Chapan
Turkmen. Dignitary's silk or velvet winter coat with weft ikat floral motifs and fur or quilted lining.

Chekman
Camel or sheep fleece coat lined with silk or cotton, worn by Turkmen people.

Chikan kari
White embroidery on white fabric from Dacca; with predominantly floral design executed on fine cotton with untwisted threads of white cotton or silk.

Chogha
Embroidered woollen men's coat from Kashmir.

Chola
Sindh. Embroidered and mirror-decorated woman's silk tunic.

Choli
Tight bodice worn with a full skirt or under a sari by women of northern India.

Chuba
Double-breasted robe worn by Tibetan officials.

Chuga
Man's long loose-fitted coat used as a court dress.

Chyrpy, chorpy
Turkmen. Tekke woman's embroidered silk mantle worn over the head, with false sleeves on the back. Silk embroideries of flowers, shrubs and hooked leaves in *kedi* stitch.

Dhoti
A rectangular length of cotton tied to form loose trousers, worn by Hindu men.

Dofuku
Wide-sleeved robe worn by monks over the *kimono*.

Dolpari
Nineteenth-century head-wear from Delhi decorated with silver strips and embroideries, which in white became the emblem of Indian nationalists.

Dorjey
Tibetan pronged ritual tool (*vajra*) made of copper and metal, showing lotus petals and fierce heads; symbol of the strongest force in the universe and symbol of the universal compassion of enlightened beings.

Doshalo
Kutch. Man's cotton wedding shawl decorated with embroideries and mirrors.

Dringin-Java
Court belt from Surakarta.

Dupatta
Women's headscarf made from two pieces of fabric sewn together, nowadays worn draped over the shoulders.

Eri
Raw silk from eastern India.

Ezar
Kutch: tie-dye printed and embroidered baggy women's trousers in satin silk.

Farrukh Sahi
Moghul Emperor who gave his name to the *angarkho* robe.

Fuku-sa
Finely decorated silk square cloth, used to wrap presents; ultimately used as handbags.

Furisode
Long-sleeved *kimono* worn by young unmarried girls.

Furoshiki
Finely decorated rectangular silk fabric used to wrap the presents for the bride.

Futema
Name given to human and animal motifs, applied to sarongs of Timor with supplementary woollen yarns.

Futon
Japanese beds.

Fuya
Bark cloth. Fabric made from a fibrous plant, usually bast, by people from Sulawesi, which is flattened and felted by soaking and beating.

Gaghra
Embroidered full skirt worn by women of western India.

Gajji
Satin silk tie-dye printed turban cloth from Gujarat.

Gauze
Fine, open, plain weave cotton or silk fabric used for summer clothes.

Geringsing
Sacred double *ikat* textile woven only in one village, Tenganan Pageringsingan, Bali.

Gresik-Java
Silk belt with metallic and silk weft threads.

Halili petondu
Ceremonial tunic with coloured cotton, beads and mica applications; worn by Kaili people from Sulawesi.

Hamam
Traditional Turkish public baths.

Hanten
Short winter tunic worn by Japanese workers during the Edo period.

Haori
Japan. Short vegetable fibre coat worn by pilgrims visiting Shinto shrines.

Happi
Short tunics worn by Japanese merchant's workers with the name of the shop painted on the back, collar and breast.

Hatta
Palestine. Bedouin's headscarf, usually in brocaded silk with tassels.

Hinggi
Man's ceremonial garment from Sumba decorated using warp ikat technique.

Inro
Small, expensively decorated Japanese medicine box.

Jaal
Floral embroidery pattern from Kashmir.

Jama
Brocaded and embroidered ceremonial dress for Hindu men with tight fitted bodice, long sleeves and heavy skirt gathered around the waist.

Jamdani
Technique for weaving fine cotton muslins from Dacca or Varanassi.

Jifu
Semi-formal brocaded (*kesi*) Chinese court robe.

Jumlo
Kohistan. Women's cotton robe decorated with a variety of items and embroideries. The heavy skirt contains between three and five hundred stitched triangles.

Kachali
Backless blouse decorated with applications, buttons and mirrors worn by Banjara people.

Kaftan
Long outer garment with long sleeves worn by men and women from Ottoman Turkey and adopted by the Islamic world. Made of brocaded silk with silk or metal needlework decorations on the borders. Open at the front, the garment has thread-covered buttons and a lining.

Kain buri
Dayak's people cotton ceremonial skirt decorated with split shells and human and *aso* motifs.

Kain kebat
Ceremonial cotton sarong decorated with sequins and beadworks and worn by Iban Dayak people.

Kain manik
Flat, rectangular wrapper cloth.

Kain panjang
"Long coat" refers to a rectangular *batik* textile wrapped around the hips (*sarong*); two and a half times as long as its width.

Kain plangi
Silk shawl from Palembang made by tritik technique (*tie-dyeing*).

Kain prada
Balinese dancer's wrapper decorated with gold leaf or dust.

Kain songket
Silk and metallic supplementary weft from Palembang.

Kaji banten
Japanese fireman's coat made of different quilted layers of cotton fabric.

Kajibaori
Late nineteenth-century Japanese woollen fire-coat with belt and chest-protector, all decorated with felt applications.

Kakaletau
Anthropomorphic patterns representing spirits and ancestors of Dayak people.

Kalati
Philippines. Small mother-of-pearl circles sewn on garments to give magical protection.

Kalka
Bean-like motifs found on Bengali embroideries.

Kamben cerek
Balinese cotton breast or shoulder cloth made by spaced-weaving technique.

Kantha
Bengali cover made of different layers of old cotton quilted and embroidered with village scenes.

Kaori
Court popular kimono worn during the Momoyama period (1573-1603), which preceded the *haori*.

Karakalpak
Central Asian people from Turkistan.

Kasuri
Name of Japanese warp-and-weft ikat technique.

Katazome
Japanese block-printing technique.

Kebaya
Java woman's blouse in fine embroidered cotton muslin.

Kemben
Silk and cotton *batik* breast-cloth worn by women from Surakarta.

Kesa
Buddhist priest's apron in silk brocade, symbolizing the Buddhist vow of poverty.

Kesi
Name given to the silk tapestry weave technique employed in China and Tibet using silk and gold wrapped threads.

Khalat
Bukhara. Wide, brocaded or ikatted overcoat secured with a belt, worn by men and women.

Khatri aba
Woman's wedding dress from Gujarat with gold thread decorations.

Khit and chok
Thai. Discontinuous supplementary weft woven by lifting out the warp by hand.

Khrorgyal
Cruel god feared by Tibetan Buddhists.

Kilim
Middle Eastern and Central Asian technique for weaving carpets and textiles, similar to European tapestry weave.

Kimishek
Karakalpak woman's bridal head-dress, with a special woollen front opening. Back is in silk ikat with embroideries and fringes.

Kimono
The principal Japanese garment worn both by men and women, cut from a piece of fabric twelve or thirteen metres long by thirty-six centimetres wide. The kimono is wrapped around the body and secured with a sash (*obi*).

Kinkhab
Heavy silk fabric, brocaded with silver and gold. Varanasi is the traditional production centre for kinkhab cloths.

Kinran
Silk warp and gold weft brocade fabric used to make the *kesa* apron.

Krang krang
Balinese woman's breast-cloth made of cotton by spaced-weaving technique.

Ku
Chinese women's trousers worn under coat.

Kuchak
Long sash worn over trousers and rolled several times.

Kurta
Bukhara. Woman's loose silk upper garment with warp *ikat* motifs. Man's loose muslin tunic shirt from northern India.

Leheria, laharia
India, Rajasthan. Resist-dyeing technique showing multicoloured stripes in wave or check effects.

Lemba
Sacred tunic in bark-cloth decorated with hand-paintings; worn by women from Sulawesi.

Limar
Silk shawl worn by Muntok Bangka island people.

Lishui
Embroidered patterns in oblique bands showing waves of the "Universal Ocean".

Long pao
Dragon-decorated robes worn by nobility and the civil service during the Qing period, the dragon being the symbol of imperial authority.

Longyi
Tube skirt with supplementary silk weft worn by Burmese.

Lungi
Textile traditionally used as a turban in Sindh and as a waistcloth in Punjab.

Makrama
Ottoman. Linen embroidered covering cloth originally used to cover meals, etc.; it gradually changed and became a woman's head covering.

Mandala
Visual representation of the universe, portraying Buddhist deities or symbols in hierarchical order; made and used in acts of Buddhist worship.

Manu obi
Precious *obi* worn with the nuptial *kimono*.

Mecit entari
Ottoman. Long dress, usually in bro-

caded silk with gold thread decorations and very long sleeves.

Mega mundung
Name of a cloud or rock-like batik design from Java.

Mendil yazma makrama
Handkerchief in printed linen and overembroidered.

Mocchi
Professional male embroiderers from Kutch famed for their delicate air-work silk embroidery.

Mon
Block-printed, white family coat-of-arms, one on each shoulder and each sleeve and one in the middle of the back.

Montsuki
Kimono bearing the family coat-of-arms.

Mothara
Rajasthan. Diagonal tie-dye decoration on men's cotton turbans in Rajasthan.

Muga
Raw silk from Eastern India.

Muna-ate
Woollen chest-piece of Japanese fire-coat (*kajibaori*).

Munahimo
Hidden cords used to secure the *kimono* from inside.

Naab
Men's striped cotton waistcoat decorated with glass beads and worn by people from Luzon.

Nussa
Sea-shells used to decorate garments all over the Indonesian archipelago.

Obi
Sash used to secure the *kimono* round the body, measuring two to three metres long by twenty-five to thirty-five centimetres wide.

Odhni
Silk or cotton cloth worn by women as a shawl over the skirt *gaghra*. It covers the head and right shoulder.

Ohenro-gi
Japan. Shikoku island pilgrims's coat covered with stamps of the shrines visited.

Oya
Ottoman. Needlework done by women for shawl edgings.

Pag
Tie-dye printed cotton muslin turbans worn by men in Rajasthan.

Paithani
High-quality saris from Maharashtra.

Pakhta
Central Asian name for cotton.

Pallav - pallu
Ends of *odhni* or *sari*, usually decorated.

Pao
Manchu woman's informal domestic silk robe (*kesi*).

Paporito noling
Toraja. Ceremonial cotton cloth with warp ikat geometric motifs.

Parang rusang
Special *batik* motif for royal clothes from Java.

Pashmina
Woollen shawl from Kashmir.

Patolu (pl. **patola**)
Silk sari woven in Gujarat by the double *ikat* technique; may be used as a wedding sari.

Peshwaj
Richly embroidered ceremonial skirt worn over trousers.

Peskir
Ottoman. Bath towel, often in linen and embroidered with silver strips.

Pha biang
Lao. Women's shoulder wrapper.

Pha sin
Thai. Tubular women's skirt (*sarong*) made of several pieces of fabric sewn together.

Phulkari
(*Flower work*) Woman's cotton shawl from Punjab with floss silk embroidery; when completely embroidered the phulkari is called bagh (*garden*), with satin or stem stitch.

Phulkari chamdan
Phulkari with the moon motif.

Phulkari sainchi
Phulkari showing scenes of peasant's life.

Phur-bu or **purba**
Ritual Tibetan Buddhist dagger showing three blades, three fierce faces and six arms – the only force capable of destroying evil.

Pua kumbu
Iban (Borneo). Ceremonial blanket dyed in rust colour taken from *Morinda citrifolia*.

Puereria
Vegetable fibre from China looking like linen.

Pukhang
Woman's skirt with cotton warp and woollen weft, worn by Kashin people from Burma.

Pulu
See *stod-gag*.

Ragi hotang
Ceremonial shawl worn by Toba Batak people.

Ragidup
Sumatra, Toba Batak. Sacred and prestige cloth woven with silk warp and cotton weft.

Ruyi
Name given to certain embroidery designs.

Sampiran
Minangkabau women's ceremonial silk head-dress.

Sape manik
Cotton ceremonial skirt decorated with beads showing dragon-like creatures, worn by Dayak people.

Sari
Cloth worn by Indian women around the waist and draped over the shoulder.

Sarong
Rectangular cloth sewn into a tube, worn throughout Indonesia by men and women.

Sashiko
Japanese embroidery stitch applied on quilted textiles.

Sati
The Sanskrit name for sari, meaning breadth of cloth.

Sehra
Valuable face-cover worn by men of noble families on their wedding day.

Selimut
General term applied to large mantles and loincloths from Timor.

Shalwar
Baggy trousers, tight at the ankle, worn by Moslem women from India, Central Asia and the Middle East.

Sheyraz
Woven or embroidered silk galloons sewn on borders of Central Asian coats (*khalat*).

Shibori
Japanese name for tie-dye motifs.

Shogun
Head of a Japanese military dictatorship; with the Emperor as head of state.

Sisha
Mirrored glass or mica used in embroidery work.

Slendang
Narrow rectangular shawl worn as breast or shoulder-cloth.

Songket
South-East Asian term for supplementary weft; the metallic thread being the major element of the supplementary weft.

Stod-gag
Tibetan Buddhist man's vest made of different pieces of brocade; yoke has a dark red large woollen band called *pulu*.

Sumi
Japan. Hand-painted ink-drawings.

Suzani
Luxurious Central Asian wall hanging, used for weddings and bed sprays. Embroidered with flower or fruit motifs (pomegranate is a symbol of fertility) in chain and Bukhara stitch.

Tai
Ethnic group, speaking many dialects of Tai language.

Tapis
Ceremonial cotton and silk *sarong* made of several panels with supplementary weft and warp ikat techniques, running stitch embroidery of

complex and fantastic creatures, worn by women in the Lampong area of southern Sumatra.

Tauranwari jooti
Woman's shoes decorated with wool tufts from Sindh.

Tekat
Gold thread embroidery of Malay origin.

Telia rumal
Square double *ikat* head-cloth or loin-cloth from Andra Pradesh.

Thirma
Woman's cotton shawl (*pulkhari*) with geometric silk embroidery.

Thob
Syria. Peasant woman's cotton embroidered dress.

Tirtanadi
Balinese open-work shawl with human supplementary weft motifs.

Toile perse
Term used in Europe in the seventeenth and eighteenth centuries to designate painted and printed cottons from India and Persia.

Tritik
Process of developing a design by binding the fabric with sewing techniques, such as tucking and gathering, before dyeing.

Tsutsugaki
Japanese *batik* technique.

Tussah
Finest of the East Indian silks.

Twill tapestry
Weaving technique. The fabric has wefts which are inserted locally to create designs. The fabric has no wefts carried from selvage to selvage. In a twill tapestry the fabric is woven in twill weave, usually a 2/2 twill, so that wefts float over and under two threads from the warp in a staggered succession.

Umbak bolong
Striped long cotton shawl from Lombok, decorated with coins.

Umpak
Cotton blouse covered with circles of mother-of-pearl and worn by people from Kulama in the Philippines.

Vajra
Buddhist's ritual wavy-bladed knife with the figures of the *makara* sea monster and flames.

Wadasan
Java, Ceriban. Special *batik* design for Japanese.

Waitao
Han. Semi-formal woman's brocaded silk surcoat.

Wheel-ships
Term used in Indian English meaning train.

Xie
Block-heel embroidered shoes worn by Guangxu women (called flower-pot).

Yama
God of hell feared and worshipped by Buddhists.

Yatak
Light Central Asian summer coat (*khalat*) made of cotton.

Yelek
Embroidered Syrian woman's cotton coat. Ottoman. Man's decorated waistcoat.

Zari
Gold and silver strip decoration. Metal thread embroidery.

Zoroaster
A community which shared the belief of the Persian prophet Zoroaster that mankind contains both good and evil in equal proportions.

Bibliography

Middle East

Al-Samih Abu Omar Abed, *Traditional Palestinian Embroidery and Jewelry*, Al-Shark Arab Press, Gerusalemme 1987.

Black David & Loveless Clive, *Islemeler: Ottoman Domestic Embroideries*, David Black Oriental Carpets, 1978.

Chevalier Dominique, *Villes et Travail en Syrie du XIXe au XXe siècle*, Paris 1982.

Gentles Margaret, *Turkish and Greek Island Embroideries*, Chicago 1964.

Gorsu Nevber, *The Art of Turkish Weaving, Designs through the Ages*, Istanbul 1988.

Lindisfarne-Tapper Nancy, Ingham Bruce, *Languages of Dress in the Middle East*, Richmond, Surrey 1997.

Pignol A., Bouajina N., Bouhalfaya J. *Costume et Parure dans le Monde Arabe*, IMA/Edifra, Paris 1987.

Senturk Sennur (edited by), *"kumas'k" Examples from the Yapi Kredi Collection of Embroidery*, Yapi Kredi Kultur Sanat, Yayincilik 1999.

Taylor Roderick, *Ottoman Embroidery*, Uta Huelsey, Wesel 1993.

Tezcan Hulya, Delibas, The Topkapi Saray Museum, *Costumes, embroideries and other Textiles*, Boston 1986.

Tezcan Hulya, *Ottoman Textiles and Embroideries*, Horhor Sanat Galerisi, 1991.

Volger Gisela, von Welck Karin, Hackstein Katharina, *Kleidung und Schmuck aus Palestina und Jordanien*, Pracht und Geheimnis, Köln 1987.

Weir Shelagh, *Palestinian Costume*, British Museum, London 1989.

Wulf Hans, *The Traditional Crafts of Persia. Their development, Technology, and Influence on Eastern and Western Civilizations*, Cambridge, Massachusetts 1966.

Turquie. Au nom de la tulipe, Editions de l'Albaron. Societe Presence du Livre, Centre culturel de Boulogne-Billancourt 1993.

Central Asia

Beresneva L., *Decorative and Applied Art of Turkmenia*, Aurora Art Publishers Leningrad 1976.

Blackwell B., *Ikat, Woven Silks from Central Asia*, Oxford 1988.

Klimburg Max & Pinto Sandra, *Tessuti Ikat dell'Asia Centrale di collezioni italiane*, Umberto Allemandi & C., Torino 1986.

Paiva R., B. Dupaigne, *Afghan Embroidery*, Musée de l'Homme, Fondation de France, Paris 1993.

The Decorative Arts of Central Asia, Zamana Gallery, London 1988.

Erben der Seidentrass, Usbekistan, Stuttgart 1995.

Muziek voor de ogen. Textiel van de volkeren uit Centraal - Azie. Music for the eyes Textile from the peoples of Central Asia, Luc Denys, Hessenhuis, Antwerpen 1997.

India

Air India Testi Originali 1976. *Sringar. Costumi dell'India*, Museo Nazionale della Montagna, Torino 1982.

Askari N., Crill R., *Colours of the Indus. Costume and Textiles of Pakistan*, Merrell Holberton in association with V. & A. Museum, London 1997.

Askari N., Arthur L., *Uncut Cloth. Saris, Shawls and Sashes*, Merrell Holberton Publishers Ltd, 1999.

Berinstain V., *Phulkari, fleurs brodées du Punjab*, AEDTA, Paris 1991.

Bonaventura P., Stockley B., *Woven Air. The Muslin & Kantha Tradition of Bangladesh*, White Chapel Art Gallery, London 1988.

Cavy V., "L'héritage du sari", in *Les nouvelles de l'Inde*, May-June, Paris 1993.

Chandra Mohanty B., Krishna K. *Ikat Fabrics of Orissa and Andhra Pradesh. Study of Contemporary Textile Crafts of India*, Calico Museum of Textiles, Ahmedabad 1974.

Cindai. Pengembaraan Kain Patola India, Jakarta 1988.

Crill R., *Indian Embroidery*. Victoria & Albert Museum, London 1999.

Denys L., *Ikat. Internationale textieltentoonstelling*, Hoofd educatieve dienst van de musea, Antwerpen 1991.

Desai C., *Ikat Textiles of India*, Thames and Hudson, London 1989.

Dhamija J., *Crafts of Gujarat. Living traditions of India*, Mapin Int. Inc., New York 1985.

Dhamija J., Jain J. (edited by), *Handwoven Fabrics of India*, Mapin Publishing Pvt. Ltd., Ahmedabad 1989.

Dhamija J., *The Woven Silks of India*, Marg Publication, Bombay 1995.

Fisher N. (edited by), *Mud, Mirror and Thread. Folk Traditions of Rural India*, Mapin, Ahmedabad in collaboration with Museum of New Mexico Press, Santa Fe 1993.

Gillow J., Barnard N., *Traditional Indian Textiles*, Thames and Hudson, London & New York 1991.

Irwin J., Hall M., *Indian Embroideries*, Calico Museum, Ahmedabad 1973.

Kennett F., *World dress. A comprehensive guide to the folk costume of the world*, Mitchell Beazley, 1994.

Nabholz-Kartaschoff, *Golden Sprays and Scarlet Flowers, Traditionnal Indian Textiles from the Museum of Ethnology, Basel.* Kyoto 1986.

Rivers V.Z., *The Shining Cloth. Dress and Adornment that Glitters*, Thames and Hudson, London 1999.

Talwar K., Krishna K., *Indian Pigment Paintings on Cloth*, Calico Museum, Ahmedabad.

Woven Air, the Muslin & kantha Tradition of Bengladesh, Whitechapel Art Gallery, London 1988.

South East Asia

Adams B.S., *Traditional Bhutanese Textiles*, White Orchid Press, 1984.

Buhler A., Nabholz M.L., *Indian Tye and Dyed Fabrics*, Calico Museum, Ahmedabad 1980.

Campbell M., *From the Hands of the Hills*, Sherry Brydson, 1978

Canuto P., Aromando E. *Tessuti Indonesiani*, Galleria Textiles and Decorative Arts, Torino 1984.

Casal G., Trotajose R., *People and Art of the Philippines*, UCLA, Museum of Cultural History, 1981.

Diran R.K., *The Vanishing Tribes of Burma*, Weidenfeld & Nicolson, London 1997.

Gavin T., *The Women's Warpath: Iban Ritual Fabrics from Borneo*, UCLA. Fowler Museum of Cultural History, University of California, Los Angeles 1996.

Gittinger M., *Splendid Symbols. Textiles and tradition in Indonesia*, Textile Museum, Washington 1979.

Hauser-Schaublin B., Nabholz-Dartaschoff M.L., Ramseyer U., *Textiles in Bali.*, Periplus Editions, Berkeley-Singapore 1991.

Heringa R., Harmen Veldhuisen C., *Fabric of Enchantment: Batik from the North Coast of Java*, Weatherhill Inc., Los Angeles, in collaborazione con Los Angeles County Museum of Art, 1996.

Homgren R.J., Spertus A.E., *Early Indonesian Textiles frim Three Island Cultures: Sumba, Toraja, Lampung*, The Metropolitan Museum of Art, New York 1989.

Howard M.C.*, Textiles of Southeast Asia. An Annotated & Illustrated Bibliography*, White Lotus Co. Ltd., Bangkok 1994.

Hunt Kahlenberg M. (edited by), *Textile Traditions of Indonesia*, Los Angeles County Museum of Art, Los Angeles 1977.

Kahn Majlis B., *Indonesische Textilien. Wege zu Göttern und Ahnen*, R.J.M. für Völkerkunde, Köln 1984.

Kahn Majlis B., *Woven Messages. Indonesian Textile Tradition in Course of Time*, Roemer-Museum, Hildesheim 1991.

Kanomi T., *People of Myth: Textiles and Crafts of the Golden Triangle*, Shikosha Publishing Co. Ltd. - Karinsha Co. Ltd, 1991.

Langewis L., Wagner F.A. *Decorative Art in Indonesian Textiles*, C.P.J. van der Peet A'dam, 1964.

Larsen, Bühker, Solyom, *Dyer's Art. Ikat – Batik – Plangi*, Van Nostrand Reinhold, 1976.

Leigh-Theisen H., Mittersakschmoeller R., *Lebens Muster. Textilien in Indonesien.* Museum für Voelkerkunde, Wien 1995.

McCabe E.I., *Batik. Fabled cloth of Java*, Viking, 1985.

Newman T.R., *Contemporary Southeast asian arts and crafts*, Crown, New York 1977.

Prangwatthanakun S., Cheesman P., *Lan Na Textiles*, Yuan Lue Lao, 1988.

Sibeth A., *Mit den Ahnen leben Batak Menschen in Indonesiên*, H. Mayer, Stuttgart-London 1990.

Solyom B., Solyom G., *Fabric Traditions of Indonesia*, Washington State University Press, Pullman e Museum of Art, Washington State University, Washington 1984.

Summerfield A., Summerfield J., *Fabled Cloths of Minangkabau*, Santa Barbara Museum of Art, Santa Barbara 1991.

Wassing-Visser R., *Weefsels en Adat Kostuums uit Indonesië*, Volkenkundig Museum Nusantara, Delft.

Bathik. Simboli magici e tradizione femminile a Giava, Electa, Milano 1988.

Far East

Buisson S., Buisson D., *Kimono – Art traditionnel du Japon*, Lausanne 1983.

Camma S., *China Dragon robes*, New York 1952.

Camma S., *Dieux et Démons de l'Himalaya, Art du bouddhisme tibétain*, Grand Palais, Paris 1977.

China House Gallery, *Catalogue – Richly Woven Traditions Costumes of the Miao of Southwest China and Beyond*, New York 1988.

Elisseff D., Elisseff V., *La civilisation japonaise. Les grandes civilisation*, Paris 1987.

Frank B., *Le panthéon bouddhique au Japon*, Collection d'Emile Guimet, Musée national des Arts asiatiques Guimet, Paris 1991.

Frederic L., *Les dieux du bouddhisme-guide iconographque*, Paris 1992.

Frick Art Museum, *Mingei Japanese folk art*, catalogue of the Montogomery Collection, Pittsburgh 1995.

Gao H., *Soieries de Chine*, Paris 1987.

Gostelow M., *Livre de la Broderie*, Dessin et Tobra, 1978.

Huang S., *Ethnic costume from Guizhou, Clothing Designs and Decorations from Minority*, Etnhic Groups in southwest in China, Beijing 1987.

Hyoso G., *Japanese design and patterns – Clasical Weaving Art*, Kyoto 1989.

Japan House Gallery, *Kosode 16th – 19th Century Textiles from Nomura Gallery*, Japan Society and Kodansha International, 1984.

Kenichi K., *Kimono – Japanese dress*. Tourist Library, vol 3. Tokyo 1956.

Kennedy A., Hosoda S., *Traditional costumes and textiles of Japan*, AEDTA, Paris 2000.

Khoo Y.E., *The straits Chinese a cultural history*, Amsterdam-Kuala Lumpur 1988.

Leavitt J.E.E., *The Silworm and the Dragon*, University of Arizona, Tucson 1986.

Life of the Emperors and Empresses in the Forbidden City, China Travel and Tourism Press, Beijing.

Musée Royal de Mariemont, *On mani padme hum*, 1977.

Musée Royal de Mariemont, *La Chine au fil de la soie. Technique, style et société au XIXᵉ siècle*, exhibition catalogue, 23 September - 20 November, Mariemont 1988.

Musée National d'Histoire Naturelle, *Trésors du Tibet – Région autonome du Tibet Chine*, Paris 1987.

National Palace Museum (edited by), *Masterpieces of Chinese Tibetan Buddhist Altar Fitting in the National Palace*, Taipeh 1971.

The Newark Museum, *Catalogue of Tibetan collection and other Lamaist Articles*, New Jersey 1950.

Noma S., *Japanese Costume and Textile Arts*, Publ. Weatherhill, New York 1974.

Noppe C., Du Castillon M.-F., Lauwaert F., *La Chine au fil de la soie. Techniques, styles et société du XIXᵉ siècle*, Musée Royal de Mariemont, Mariemont 1988.

Rawson P., *Sacerd Tibet*, London 1991.

Royal Academy of Arts, *Catalogue – The Great Japan Exhibition- Art of Edo Period 1600-1868*.

Sadao H., *Japanese detail fashion*, San Francisco 1989.

Saome Jenyns R., Lion-Goldschmidt D., *Arts de la Chine – Soieries et tapis, Verre, Ivoire, Pierres dures, Flacons à tabac, Pierre à encre et autres objets*, Office du Livre 1980.

Simcox J., *Chinese Textiles*, Spink & Son Ltd., London 1994.

Snellgrove D.L., Richardson H.E., *A cultural history of Tibet*. Boston-London 1968.

The Art Iinstitute of Chicago Museum Studies, *Clothed to Rule the Universe Ming and Qing Dynasty Textiles at the Art of Institute of Chigago*, vol. 26, n. 2, Chigago 2000.

Vollmer J.E., *Chinese costume and Accessories 17th - 20th century*, AEDTA, Paris 1999.

Vollmer J.E., *In the jusense of the dragon throne: Ch'ing dynasty costume 1644-1911*, Royal Ontario Museum, Torronto 1977.

Wang Yi Wang Shuqing, Lu Yanzhen, *Daily Life in the Forbidden City, The Qing dynasty 1644-1912*, Hong Kong 1985.

Wang Y., *Chinese folk Embroidery*, London 1987.

Wilson V., *Chinese Dress*, Victoria & Albert Museum, London 1986.

Wrigglesworth L., *The Purse*, 1988.

Yarong W., *Chinese Folk Embroidery*, Thames and Hudson, London 1987.

Yuchi Z., Kuang S., *Clothings and Ornaments of China's Miao People*, Tan Cultural Palace of Nationalities, Beijing 1985.

Zhou X., Chunming G., *Le Costume Chinois*, Office du Livre, Fribourg 1985.

Index